Contents

ENCOUNTERING THE DEPTHS

MOTHER MARY CLARE, S.L.G.

ENCOUNTERING THE DEPTHS

Edited by Ralph Townsend

Foreword by
Bishop Michael Ramsey

Darton, Longman and Todd
London

First published in 1981
Darton, Longman & Todd Ltd
89 Lillie Road
London SW6 1UD

ISBN 0 232 51510 7

British Library Cataloguing in Publication Data

Mary Clare, *Mother*
   Encountering the depths.
   1. Devotion
   I. Title
   248.3   BV4815

   ISBN 0-232-51510-7

Phototypeset by Input Typesetting Ltd., London SW19 8DR
Printed in Great Britain by The Anchor Press Ltd
and bound by Wm Brendon & Son Ltd
both of Tiptree, Essex

Foreword

I hope this little work will have many readers, as I am sure it will help them as it has helped me. Christian people are often shy of contemplation, thinking it to be an exercise which is beyond them or a practice suitable for monks and nuns or an escape from the practical needs of the world. Contemplation is none of these things. It is a liberation from our restless brain-activity into the depth of the love of God in our souls, a love which brings us nearer to the needs of the world around us.

Can I achieve this? It is not a matter of our achieving, but of the opening of our heart to receive the gift which God will pour into it. Christian lives which know contemplation will be lives nearer the love of God in its outflowing stream.

+ Michael Ramsey

Editor's Preface

Mother Mary Clare is a theologian in the orthodox sense of the word: she is concerned not with working through abstract concepts but with contemplation. She recognizes that the roots of theology are implanted in ordinary living, and that human experience is a mystery which raises man up to God. Her approach to prayer and contemplation will therefore appeal to all sorts of people: not only to those who like herself have obeyed the call to the cloister and to other 'professional' theologians, but also to those of us who approach the Christian life with little or no formal academic theological training. The mark of her integrity and the authenticity of her theology is that she abolishes the superficial differences between one way of living in the Church and another – there is only one call.

Most of the material used in this book has been published elsewhere, but some of it has come from Mother Mary Clare's more personal writings. The chapter headings were suggested naturally by the themes in her writing, and my task has been only to shape the original disparate material into a form of spiritual narrative. Because most of the material was originally written and delivered as lectures there has been some alteration in style, but it has been my utmost care not to obscure the remarkable clarity and forthrightness which so faithfully express the quality of her own response to the call to seek God. A number of quite lengthy passages from Scripture are reproduced in the text in order that reading the book may itself encourage readers to engage in precisely the practice wherein Mother Mary Clare locates the origin of true contemplation – in brooding upon the Scriptures.

The House of SS Gregory   RALPH TOWNSEND
   and Macrina,
Oxford,
September 1980

Acknowledgements

The author gratefully acknowledges the kind permission given by S. L. G. Press, Fairacres, Oxford, to reproduce in this book much of the material already published in a different form in their series of pamphlets on spirituality, and she is very grateful that the Press will continue to publish the original pamphlets. Most of the contents of these pamphlets were originally delivered as lectures to Roman Catholic religious at the invitation of the Warden of Spode House, Staffordshire, the Rev. Conrad Peppler, O.P. These occasions she regards as enormously valuable ecumenical encounters. Moreover, she gratefully acknowledges the depth of experience given her by the many clergy, ordinands and lay-people who have come to the Sisters of the Love of God in their search for unity of life through prayer. And finally she is indebted to the community itself for giving her the opportunity to share in its ministry.

Biblical quotations are taken from the New English Bible (N.E.B.), Second Edition © 1970, by permission of Oxford and Cambridge University Presses; and from the Jerusalem Bible published and © 1966, 1967 and 1968 by Darton, Longman & Todd Ltd and Doubleday & Co. Inc., and used by the permission of the publishers.

The quotations from the works of St John of the Cross are taken from *S. John of the Cross: Complete Works*, tr. Allison Peers (Burns, Oates & Washbourne 1947) and *The Poems of S. John of the Cross*, tr. Roy Campbell (Harvill Press, 8th edn 1972).

CHAPTER ONE

The Search for a Relationship

Where there is a deep humility thither comes the Holy
Ghost; when the grace of the worshipful spirit comes,
the man under its influence is filled with all purity.
Then he sees God and God too looks on him.

St Simeon the New Theologian

Prayer is the gateway to the vision of God for which we
were created. It is the means for free and conscious in-
tercourse between the creature and his creator, and it
expresses the union between the two. It is the art of
spiritual living, and it will be incomplete if it includes
only the presence of God without the necessary complement of the presence of man. It is an entirely false dichotomy which distinguishes between prayer as a purely
Godward or personal activity on the one hand, and on
the other as a compassionate involvement with the
world's pain, insecurity and frustration which would seem
to make prayer in the old, traditional sense of the word
irrelevant. When we pray, we are being united with Jesus
Christ in his own redemptive action; we are being drawn
into the great cosmic battle against evil, which is to bring
into the here and now of our daily lives the fruits of
Christ's victorious passion.

Seen in this light, it is strange that we all find it difficult
to recognize the urgency of prayer; nor are we prepared
to face the cost of prayer. Yet, of course, this is no

modern problem:

Six days later Jesus took Peter, James and John with him and led them up a high mountain where they were alone; and in their presence he was transfigured; his clothes became dazzling white, with a whiteness no bleacher on earth could equal. They saw Elijah appear, and Moses with him, and there they were conversing with Jesus. Then Peter spoke: 'Rabbi', he said, 'how good it is that we are here! Shall we make three shelters, one for you, one for Moses, and one for Elijah?' (For he did not know what to say; they were so terrified.) Then a cloud appeared, casting its shadow over them, and out of the cloud came a voice: 'This is my Son, my Beloved; listen to him.' And now suddenly, when they looked around, there was nobody to be seen but Jesus alone with themselves.

On their way down the mountain, he enjoined them not to tell anyone what they had seen until the Son of Man had risen from the dead. They seized upon these words, and discussed among themselves what this 'rising from the dead' could mean. And they put a question to him: 'Why do our teachers say that Elijah must come first?' He replied, 'Yes, Elijah does come first to set everything right. Yet how is it that the scriptures say of the Son of Man that he is to endure great sufferings and to be treated with contempt? However, I tell you, Elijah has already come, and they have worked their will upon him, as the scriptures say of him.'

When they came back to the disciples they saw a large crowd surrounding them and lawyers arguing with them. As soon as they saw Jesus the whole crowd were overcome with awe, and they ran forward to welcome him. He asked them, 'What is this argument about?' A man in the crowd spoke up: 'Master, I brought my son to you. He is possessed by a spirit which makes him speechless. Whenever it attacks him, it dashes him to the ground, and he foams at the mouth, grinds his teeth, and goes rigid. I asked your disciples to cast it out, but they failed.' Jesus answered: 'What an unbelieving and perverse generation! How long shall I be with you? How long must I endure you? Bring him to me.' So they brought the boy to him; and as soon as the spirit saw him it threw the boy into convulsions, and he fell on the ground and rolled about foaming at the mouth. Jesus asked his father: 'How long has he been like this?' 'From childhood,' he replied; 'often it has tried to make an end of him by throwing him into the fire or into water. But if it is at all possible for you, take pity upon us and help us.' 'If it is possible!' said Jesus. 'Everything is possible to one who has faith.' 'I have faith,' cried the boy's father; 'help me where faith falls short.' Jesus saw then that the crowd was closing in upon them, so he rebuked the unclean spirit. 'Deaf and dumb spirit,' he said, 'I command you, come out of him and never go back!' After crying aloud and racking him fiercely, it came out; and the boy looked like a corpse; in fact, many said, 'He is dead.' But Jesus took his hand and raised him to his feet, and he stood up.

Then Jesus went indoors, and his disciples asked him privately, 'Why could not we cast it out?' He said, 'There is no means of casting out this sort but prayer.'

Mark 9:2–29 (N.E.B.)

In this passage we see the disciples at the foot of the mount of Transfiguration full of apostolic zeal and awareness that they have been commissioned by the Lord to preach the good news of the Kingdom and heal the sick. They have also been commissioned to cast out devils. But when it came to the point, the boy was still helpless and still possessed by strange forces both spiritual and psychic which they were unable to dispel or heal. The occasion was one of tragedy drawing out the sympathy of the beholders and heightened because of the expectation of the parents and the disappointment of the disciples themselves at their own incapacity. On this occasion, it was not compassionate involvement that was lacking, but the dynamic power of their prayer: the disciples had been given the divine commission and doubtless they had tried to carry out the Lord's wish with all the concentration and force of their natural human energy. But this had been of no avail. In fact, what was needed was the transforming power of prayer. The prayer they had to learn was something more than carrying out a command, or seeking the intervention of divine power as a magical act. In the case of Jesus, his prayer was the complete expression of his human will and energy with the will of his Father. In Jesus, God's activity was central, operating in and through the divine humanity, unhindered. During our feeble efforts to pray, we are constantly confronted by our own imperfect faculties which obstruct the complete co-operation with the spirit of God which is the essence of prayer. It is the prayer of the 'just man made perfect' that is of power.

The first lesson we have to learn about prayer is that it is God's activity in us, and not a self-activated process of our own. The Desert Fathers, those great masters of the spiritual life, knew all about the essential condition of learning to pray. They called it 'purity of heart', without which there could be no true *metanoia* or conversion. We can pray only if our hearts are truly pure in the sense

4

of Jesus' teaching in the Sermon on the Mount, where the pure in heart shall see God. Prayer and daily life are indivisible. We must learn to pray as we are, and accept ourselves as we are, and not as the ideal people we would like to imagine ourselves to be. We must grow to understand ourselves and accept that it is at the time when our natural passions are most active, and our minds most distracted, that we can grow to a knowledge of ourselves as real persons. That is the point of tension at which we must offer ourselves to God in prayer.

At the beginning of our learning to pray, therefore, we must relate prayer to conversion of life. Prayer, which is the fruit of true conversion, is an activity, an adventure, and sometimes a dangerous one, since there are occasions when it brings neither peace nor comfort, but challenge, conflict and new responsibility. This is why so many old ways of praying, and books about prayer, seem to have let us down. Too often when we used them we were hoping to get something for ourselves from prayer, perhaps security or a growing sensible realization and knowledge of God. To seek such things in prayer is a mistake. The essential heart of prayer is the throwing away of ourselves in self-oblation to God, so that he can do with us what he wills. Any form of prayer which does not incite a costing giving in love soon becomes sterile, dry and a formal duty.

Prayer is thus the search for a relationship. 'My God, if you insist, make me know you,' exclaimed Pascal, and that will be our exclamation as our inner longing for God gradually wakens to the fact that without him we are nothing. When things get to this stage in prayer, instead of thinking that something might have gone wrong with our prayer, we should recognize in it a real sign of growth, stability and maturity. It is a cause for great thanksgiving when we are prepared to make the leap of faith at the call of God into a way of prayer that may seem dark and meaningless, but which, in reality, is an invitation of love to greater intimacy. This is the reality of the situation, though we ourselves may be aware of nothing except our inability to formulate our deepest longings. In this relationship we must be childlike, believing that God knows the inner secrets of our hearts and that there is no need for us to formulate them in words.

Sometimes, rather than engage in formal meditation, it is better to make some simple, short and if possible spontaneous act of faith, hope and love. This enables us to anchor ourselves and not drift either into self-centred depression or, in the opposite direction, into a prayer which avoids contact with the darkness of reality. In the early stage of learning to pray, it is right to use our natural creative gifts, provided they are seen as means to an end, and not an end in themselves to our natural enjoyment. Some may be encouraged to use their love of poetry to express their love for God; others may find real inspiration in using reproductions of the old masters to relate the beauty of visual form to biblical and other spiritual writings in order to enliven their affective acts of prayer. But all this must be seen as a stage on the way by which the Holy Spirit leads us into the night of faith and begins to strip the soul of all dependency on natural aids to prayer. We must be ready to give up these prayerful activities and lay ourselves open to a deeper degree of purification of the faculties – a stage in which it will largely seem to us that we are doing nothing – to prepare us for the transition from activity to passivity in prayer. God thus prepares us to *be* rather than to make acts of love.

If, instead of following our formal meditations, our

schemes and techniques of prayer, we could realize the inner meaning of such phrases as 'Jesus is prayer', much of this thirst to pray would be quenched with the living water of God's love, whether we were aware of it or not. To set us praying, many of us need to relate our desire for God, for what God is and what he does in Jesus, as expressed in our private prayer, with our participation in common worship where we are all drawn into and become part of the redemptive acts of God. One of the dangers of the past has been the dichotomy between private prayer and eucharistic prayer. In reality they complement each other. One of the unspeakable benefits which all religious share, and in which all Christians can participate equally if they will, is the re-enactment of the Gospel through the words and actions of the office and the eucharist.

We must in these days take seriously the responsibility of learning to pray, because many, especially from among the younger generation, are looking to forms of non-Christian transcendental experience in their craving for experience beyond that of our normal physical and mental life. This is a modern form of false mysticism of the kind always likely to be stimulated by a promiscuous society. It manifests an unhealthy curiosity and speculation about the supranormal. We must see this against the background of the inalienable purposes of God and the eternal mysteries of the faith. The world will not be brought back to an acknowledgement of the power of Christ unless those of us who are at the praying heart of the Church have prayed back the cross and its message of love into the centre of Christian witness. By the generosity of our self-oblation, as we give ourselves to be living witnesses to the principles of sacrifice, and as we seek in prayer to be drawn into deeper union with Jesus in his passion, we shall be giving ourselves to be participators in his continuous intercession to draw us and all men into unity and into the knowledge of himself. It is not through forcing the human will but through drawing it to recognize and co-operate with the power of God expressed in love that we in the faithful following of our various vocations bear witness to the redeeming power of love. All our prayer activities must be seen as means and not ends in themselves, because they are to lead us to a relationship with Jesus.

Prayer is essentially, then, a love affair with God, not schemes or techniques or ways of prayer, but the most direct, open approach of each one of us as a person to God our creator, redeemer and sanctifier. This is something beyond all methods and ideas. We are seeking God himself, not thoughts about him, nor about ourselves in relation to him. Prayer is an adventure at the end of which we stand face to face before the living God; not in a vague way in a place we call heaven, but in the here and now of our lives, by, with and in Christ, as we are made part of his prayer and his offering to the Father through the power of the Holy Spirit. One of the real aspects of the here and now is boredom, and that too we must turn into love and sacrificial offering. These moments may be likened to the interminable letters and telephone calls that happen before any sort of permanent relationship is established in the initial stages of a love affair between a man and a woman. The important thing is that these times of communication must not be mistaken for the engagement itself, or the final oblation of each to the other in the fullness of love.

If we are straining in our prayer, or putting a wrong emphasis on our own activity in prayer, this will probably manifest itself by pressure on our nerves, from which can come lack of charity. There is often need for increased watchfulness when we are making some special spiritual effort, such as during Lent or while making a retreat. We can unintentionally put too much emphasis on our own effort and concentration, rather than on consecrated attention to God. Through psychology we now know much more than we did about the interaction of body and soul which make the whole man, and which work together in the actual process we call prayer. It is for this reason that each of our faculties must be purified and unified in order that we may be ready for the Holy Spirit to bring our prayer to fruition. There was once a time, especially in the religious life, when we were afraid of being natural, and so relaxation as a form of preparation for prayer would not have been thought of; at least certainly not in those terms. We of the older generation were trained to kneel upright with folded hands and maintain a uniform deportment through our times of prayer. This may be a necessary stage through which most of us need to go. But it is important in learning to pray that we learn first to *live* with the tensions and fears, both mental and physical, which are a part of us, and second to *use* them and let them become transformed in the deepening of our prayer life in Christ. This is very important, because we communicate anxiety and tension one to another without knowing it. So in praying we need to know how to deal with the tensions of our bodies, by adopting a posture in prayer which suits our natural temperaments. Some may pray best standing, others kneeling or prostrate on the floor, others sitting quietly relaxed in a chair with hands on knees and head upright. A concern with physical posture and the process of breathing to which it is so closely related leads us to be more aware of what our Orthodox brethren call 'learning to pray always'.

These matters of learning to pray are intimately concerned with the pervasive matter of spirituality. We must keep our own desire to pray, and the quality of our prayer, in a relation to the larger issues around us. We tend to reduce God's stature by substituting ourselves as the measure by which we judge whether or not we are fully mature and fulfilled as human beings. If spirituality may be defined as the search for a personal relationship between God and mankind, then spirituality is something which embraces the whole of man's life in the present. Independently of God, man cannot understand either himself or his environment. When he thinks and acts independently from God, he misuses his creativity; and from that misuse stems his interior conflict and disharmony, his failure in personal relationships, his despair covered up by activism, pleasure-seeking and abortive attempts at self-realization. There also follows his misuse of the natural environment which has created the present world-wide problems of pollution. Man needs to approach spirituality with a sense of alienation from his true self and his true destiny within the scheme of things. In a return to genuine dependence on God, in an acknowledgement of his own status as a son of God in union with Christ, lies the only true way to man's full maturity. In this spirituality of dependence on God lie the reconciliation and unity at all levels for which the world is crying out. We must acknowledge the supremacy of the God who works through history, the God who is at work in the present moment of history, in order that the tensions of national, church and individual life be healed.

Most religious and political philosophers today leave either the body or the spirit out of their reckoning; or they divide the two. Dialectical materialism, for example, ignores the spirit. Those who use drugs to induce mystical

10

states seek to go out from the body. Many non-Christian sects, and even some Christian ones, regard the body as evil and as an obstacle to the life of the spirit. The Christian assurance against all these problems is a system fully incarnational and sacramental. We should be living witnesses to the fact that Christianity is not esoteric but ordinary. The world should see the extraordinariness of Christianity in the family love, the sacrifice, the obedience, the mutuality made incarnate in the Christian community, in its way of personal relationships and in its way of dealing with things. Christian spirituality affirms that the thing done in the body is a true expression of the thing believed in the soul; that both the act and the belief have eternal value. Psychology, medicine, science and some religions and sects very often minimize man's moral responsibility, regarding him as the slave of physical and psychical impulses rather than as a free agent. In the face of this, Christian spirituality stresses judgement, mercy and redemption. It does not deny the discoveries which affirm the diminished responsibility of the individual for what he does in many instances, but it denies that this is the last word. Christ descends into the unconscious, and he ascends beyond our earthly conceiving. Christians must witness to the world the power of Christ to heal and change lives. The slave of Christ is a free man, witnessing to the power of the incarnate and risen God amid natural causes and disabilities in his life and his prayer. Not death, but the resurrection of the body and the transfiguration of the world is the end, and the goal, of human life.

The division between thought and action is present in every soul and in every church, but it is a division which can be bridged by the right understanding of Christian contemplative prayer. The positive answer lies in the realization of the equal value and rich uniqueness of each individual vocation within the whole Church, and this points the way to a truer realization of a fundamental unity in diversity of races, churches and nations. It is not even desirable that we should all be the same. Within the one Christ there is a great diversity of vocations, but prayer in Christ, in all its manifold forms, is the birthright of all Christian people. It is the fruit of our initiation by baptism and the Spirit into the Body of Christ. Yet again we are reminded that prayer is not a self-activated process, but a release of God's own energy, the work of the Holy Spirit in us.

> . . . the Spirit comes to the aid of our weakness. We do not even know how we ought to pray, but through our inarticulate groans the Spirit himself is pleading for us, and God who searches our inmost being knows what the Spirit means, because he pleads for God's own people in God's own way; and in everything, as we know, he co-operates for good with those who love God and are called according to his purpose.
>
> Romans 8:26–8 (N.E.B.)

We must not take this gift lightly or expect the Spirit to act magically. Prayer, like the sacraments, requires our personal co-operation and response to the Spirit. The ability to pray, to enter into communion with God, is a gift of God, an expression of his love for man, but a gift that calls for a freely-willed reception on man's part. Each person must decide whether he is willing to pay the cost of entering into a continually renewed and continually deepening relationship with God in prayer.

Prayer that is worthy of the name demands total commitment, and such a commitment demands of us a true and costing response. As a man sows, so shall he reap, and as a man lives, so shall he pray. Prayer and life, living and praying, are indivisible. In order that contemplative prayer may be truly the bringing of the Holy Spirit into the world's pain and tensions, there must be an element of costly purification. This requires positive detachment for those giving themselves seriously to the work of prayer. If prayer is learning to unite our wills with the will of God, then the cost must be the cost of Calvary. To learn to love as Christ loves is to discover through commitment the true renewing of our whole being, in God, on behalf of the world. The essential mark of Christian contemplation is its inseparability from Christ's way of reconciliation. To learn to love as Christ loves involves both vision and spiritual conflict. To let our love, our desire, our faculties be taken and transformed by Christ in the Spirit is to discover the renewing of our whole being before God. Vision is a turning to God, turning away from the world for the sake of the world, turning to God that our feebleness may be healed, purified by his holiness so that a little of his glory may be reflected in us. There can be no substitute for the deepened life of prayer and communion with God, implying both death and resurrection, an entering into the darkness of contemplation which no tongue can explain.

There are as many ways of the soul's approach to God as there are different personalities. Each must find his own particular way, assured that the one common practice for all is our knowledge of and our praying in the Bible. In the great tradition of Christian prayer, whether it be that of the Desert Fathers, or the later centuries of monastic practice in both East and West, the Bible has always been the ground of true prayer. In the West, later medieval and post-Tridentine spirituality built up more intellectual systems of prayer which many Christians to-

13

day do not find helpful. Our danger in rejecting these systems is that we run the risk of drifting into a vague, formless 'prayer', all too often and loosely called contemplative. Christian prayer must never be confused with transcendental meditation.

The Desert Fathers were prepared to repeat over and over again such affirmations of trust and dependency on God as 'O God make speed to save me, O Lord make haste to help me'. St Benedict taught his monks to make their prayer short and simple, based on the recitation of the psalms and a simple brooding on the words of the Scriptures, memorizing or reciting a verse or portion of the Bible till their minds were stilled and their hearts warmed by the constant intaking of divine truth. In this way their wills were moved to conformity with the will of God. Their reading of Scripture was carried out in great simplicity, without the aid of commentaries. Such simple prayer opens the door to a growing intimacy with God. In the simple desert prayer, Scripture was read slowly and meditatively. It was a ruminating on the words, which were pronounced with the lips as well as read with the eyes. This entrance of the words by means of both the ears and eyes meant that they were planted in the very being of the reader, and constituted a conceiving of the Word in the heart. It is a primary condition of hearing the Word that the mind be free and alert, and the heart clean and open. In this condition the Holy Spirit can bring home to the soul the message God wants it to receive; not only the literal facts or ideas, but their re-alization in the life of the reader, its fruit-bearing in his words and actions. By listening to the Word and allowing it full play in our hearts we find ourselves moved to respond. That is how true prayer is born, the brooding prayer of one who converses with God and answers his

14

prayer. The effect of this brooding and communing with God is expressed by Origen in his Homily on Psalm 36:

> Then the word of God shall have come into your souls and clinging to your hearts will form your minds according to the image of the word itself, i.e. that you should desire and do what the word of God wills, and thereby Christ himself will be formed in you.

In this connection, consider the passage in Exodus 33:

> Moses used to take a tent and pitch it at a distance outside the camp. He called it the Tent of the Presence, and everyone who sought the Lord would go out to the Tent of the Presence outside the camp. Whenever Moses went out to the tent, all the people would rise and stand, each at the entrance to his tent, and follow Moses with their eyes until he entered the tent. When he entered it, the pillar of cloud came down, and stayed at the entrance to the tent while the Lord spoke with Moses. As soon as the people saw the pillar of cloud standing at the entrance to the tent, they would all prostrate themselves, every man at the entrance to his tent. The Lord would speak with Moses face to face, as one man speaks to another. Then Moses would return to the camp, but his young assistant, Joshua son of Nun, never moved from inside the tent.
>
> Moses said to the Lord, 'Thou bidst me lead this people up, but thou has not told me whom thou wilt send with me. Thou hast said to me, "I know you by name, and further, you have found favour with me." If I have indeed won thy favour, then teach me to know thy way, so that I can know thee and continue in favour with thee, for this nation is thy own people.' The Lord answered, 'I will go with you in person and set your

mind at rest.' Moses said to him, 'Indeed if thou dost not go in person, do not send us up from here; for how can it ever be known that I and thy people have found favour with thee, except by thy going with us? So shall we be distinct, I and thy people, from all the peoples on earth.' The Lord said to Moses, 'I will do this thing that you have asked, because you have found favour with me, and I know you by name.'

Exodus 33:7–17 (N.E.B.)

There the writer speaks of the Tent of Meeting 'pitched without the camp' and 'afar off from it', placed, that is, in solitude and silence, away from the noise and bustle of the camp. As Moses enters the Tent, the pillar of cloud descends, the sign and symbol of the presence of the God who had revealed himself to Moses at Horeb, whom Moses had worshipped and obeyed. 'The Lord would speak with Moses face to face, as one man speaks to another.' In this same way we, as seekers after God, find that God gives himself to us abundantly. He first reveals himself, and if we respond in worship and obedience, if we wait upon him in silence and solitude, we enter into true conversation and communion with him. There is question and answer, command and obedient reply, a dialogue of mutual giving and receiving.

This provides us with a clue as to how to use our prayer time when it hangs heavy upon us, when we cannot concentrate, or when we are sleepy or restless; when we do not know what to say. We must give God a chance to speak, as he is the prevenient God who takes the initiative. Our dumbness and inability to speak may be the result of our not having listened to what he has to say. It is so much easier to enter into a conversation with someone who has asked a question. Then we can reply.

So, in our relation with God, we should open our Bibles and read slowly, prayerfully, and wait. Then, when God speaks to us through the words of the Bible, we will reply in true dialogue. Sometimes we might even argue with God, as Abraham, Moses and the prophets sometimes did, but ultimately, as our forefathers did, only to praise and thank him, to love him and offer ourselves in obedience to him.

It must be for each individual to determine personally what the practice of prayer means in terms of fidelity in setting aside time for prayer daily or weekly, and of perseverence in prayer when the practice seems unpalatable or meaningless. True prayer rests not in emotional experience but in steadfastness of the will to set itself only on what God desires. We must accept the fact that we shall never know the true meaning of prayer without perseverence in the act of praying itself. While it is important to realize that our brooding prayer based on Scripture feeds and makes alive our eucharistic worship, and likewise that liturgical prayer keeps our private prayer from becoming too subjective, it is one of the signs of the times that for many people, lay and ordained, the non-liturgical form of their prayer is becoming increasingly simple, still, wordless, except for very short affirmations of praise, love, penitence. Even the repetition of a single word, such as the name of Jesus, or some exclamation such as 'O God, you are my God', is sufficient to express the heart of prayer. All the desire of the heart can be breathed out in the one word 'God'.

Many today are turning to the Eastern Orthodox practice of the recitation of the Jesus Prayer: 'Jesus Christ, Son of the Living God, have mercy on me a sinner.' This prayer has the whole of theology in it, and its repetition is a good way of establishing the basis of our prayer on a firm foundation. First, there is the statement of Jesus as the Christ, the Son of God. He is Lord and God, not just another good friend, another nice person to talk to, but God and Saviour. This concept of the majesty and judgement of God is important. It really is *God* whom we worship, in whom we shall find heartbreak as well as joy, dread as well as peace, judgement as well as mercy. Second, there is the person who prays, who is alienated from God, a sinner who has fallen short of the glory of God and who sees in the face of God's majesty his own unworthiness. And third, there is in between these two, between the majestic God and the sinner, the *eleison*, the mercy and loving kindness of God. That is the basic theological fact that our whole life is to realize: God is in Christ reconciling the world to himself in us and through us, day by day. And *that* is the life of prayer. In a life of prayer, the process of re-orientation of ourselves towards God, we have to learn how to acknowledge that we are sinners; not by emotional self-deprecation, nor by psycho-analysis, though this may be a necessary way towards true self-knowledge, but by looking towards God with hands empty and open to receive his mercy. He will then lead us on to the next thing he has in store for us. In prayer, that is to say, in true theology of living, repentance does not mean misery, but genuine conversion of heart. It is the way of those often unpopular words: cross, crucifixion, asceticism, duty and rule.

If we really want to pray, we have to give time to learning its lessons. We are free to love, and every moment of the day is God's good time. We must be realistic, and give ourselves time to realize what we are truly seeking. Perhaps we all tend to worry too much about ourselves in prayer. All we really need to do is to be full of gratitude, praise and thanksgiving, and we shall be the temples in which Jesus himself will pray. Such a relationship allows God to be God and man to be man in the fullness of freedom. In this context alone are God and man bound together, and in it we discover how the process of mutual exploration which is prayer may develop.

CHAPTER TWO

The Dimension of Silence

In the deserts of the heart,
Let the Healing fountain start.
In the prison of his days,
Teach the free man how to praise
          W.H. Auden ('In Memory of W.B. Yeats')

Our society is fundamentally materialistic. The worth of the people is measured in terms of what they earn, and the value of their lives is assessed by the external activities. Many dread retirement or old age because the meaning of life for them is centred on externals, and once the possibility of activity is taken away, the reason for living is lost. Psychiatrists tell us that our mental hospitals are full because people have either never achieved or lost a really balanced inner life: their capacity for fully mature and lasting personal relationships has never developed, so for them life is purposeless, and lacks clear direction.

The choice we Christians have to make is not between the importance of God and the importance of man, for where there is no knowledge of God or belief in God there can be no true understanding of the value and dignity of man. The Christian, in choosing to place God at the centre of his life, comes to see all human life and purpose as having eternal meaning in relation to God. There is a tradition going back to Origen which says that man is what he does with his silence. There is a terror in silence if a man is conscious only of being an isolated individual. Man is made for fellowship, to be part of a family.

Although speech is a necessary means of communication, there is a whole realm of human, as well as spiritual exploration in which silence can be the medium of a positive exchange of communication. Not many people are aware of this. As a culture we are afraid to be silent. In silence there is not the same opportunity for egoism, by which much frightening emptiness can be concealed. Even in our most altruistic activity, the aggressive, power-loving ego is projected onto others, in order either to protect ourselves or to express ourselves. There can in spite of all this, however, be a sense of communication in silence. In this communication, it is God who is the link, and not something we ourselves are doing or saying. Silence can therefore be both precious, and powerful as an instrument of God's will and purpose.

Silence is not simply a matter of refraining from speech: there is a relaxed, creative silence which is a medium for spiritual affinity and unity, a union of spirits in the one aim of seeking God and seeking each other in God. The positive use of silence is important to each one of us in our life of prayer. Silence is the matrix of eternity.

Shout aloud and rejoice, daughter of Zion; I am coming, I will make my dwelling among you, says the Lord. Many nations shall come over to the Lord on that day and become his people, and he will make his dwelling with you. Then you shall know that the Lord of Hosts has sent me to you. The Lord will once again claim Judah as his own possession in the holy land, and make Jerusalem the city of his choice.

Silence, all mankind, in the presence of the Lord!

For he has bestirred himself out of his holy dwelling-
place.

Zechariah 2:10-13 (N.E.B.)

In the Gospels we see Jesus taking his exhausted disciples apart to rest in a form of prayerful withdrawal after
their busy days of active ministry: we see also that Jesus
himself found communion with the Father in the silence
of his night prayer. The Fathers of the Church, both
Eastern and Western, and the great exponents of desert
spirituality, identified this silence with charity and purity
of heart. Such silence is not content with exorcising noise;
silence is a submission of body and soul to the rhythm of
the Spirit. Silence which is not just absence of speech is
synonymous with loss of ego, with a stillness of spirit in
which the true self, made in the image and likeness of
God, may be released from the shackles of fear. In silence
we are released from our prison to know by experience
the splendour of the liberty of the children of God. In
silence God dwells in us, and we in him.

From such silence in prayer comes a stilling of the
mind. There comes a cessation of the interior chatter
which surges up from memory and the unconscious, and
which threatens to disturb our quiet attention on God.
Not that disturbance, when it occurs, should distress un-
duly. Many people are disturbed by the fact that times of
prayer may be times of genuine temptations, of psychological and even sexual fantasies. It is to be expected that
the lower levels, so often kept at bay by activity, should
come to the surface when we try to be still before God.
In silent prayer they can be faced and acknowledged in
positive affirmation, and redirected into deeper penitence, deeper silence, a simpler dependence on the Holy

Spirit. In prayer, as in life, the cleansing of memory and the stilling of the active imagination is an essential part of the purgative way. Repression is dangerous, and can be the cause of spiritual sluggishness as well as psychological disturbance. The cleansing that unifies and stills must come through the rising up of love, the desire to be wholly God's. True silence is to be found in the willingness to be wholly conformed to God's will. The silence from speech, the stilling of the memory, imagination and mind must lead ultimately to the conformity of will wherein God will ask nothing less than everything, and in which our prayer can be but an echo of the prayer in the Garden of Gethsemane: 'Thy will be done'.

What this dimension of silence means in relation to prayer is an intensely personal matter. In order that prayer may become a dialogue of love, a unity of the human heart with God, we need to rest very much on the activity of the Holy Spirit. Mother Teresa of Calcutta once said that God is the friend of silence, and that silence is that which enables the touching of souls. In the silence of waiting and expectancy God speaks through us. In Mother Teresa and her sisters, in their work with starving, dying, abandoned men, women and children, we see examples of women in whom the false self has been burnt away by the love of Christ, and in whom contemplation and activity are completely united. We have not all reached that true unity of the self in God; but through silence we have the means to recognize in ourselves our need for the emptiness of self which God may fill, substituting his love and his will for our own desires. We can recognize our need for times of withdrawal and quiet, when we can be still and let God fill us with himself. It is in that stillness that the vision is given 'without which the people perish', the vision of which the Church is in constant need if it is to be constantly renewed. In the reality of the silence of the heart, those nourished by the teaching of Christ can and do understand and communicate with each other wordlessly. This silence is the source of the prophetic power possessed by men and women of vision.

When we first enter upon the way of silence, the mere lack of noise may be more disturbing than the continuous noise of the radio or the roaring of jet planes overhead, for in the exterior silence we find inner noise cutting across the attention we desire to give to God. This need not cause very much worry, but when we become aware of it, we should return gently to the still centre of our being where God is at work imperceptibly but surely.

Silence is the doorway into the need of the world, the condition of the prayer which arises out from the heart of the universe, because it expresses the love of Christ, crucified and risen for the world. Such profound prayer, however, is not concerned only with the world as a whole, but also with the most mundane details of our ordinary, everyday lives. Prayer is not a part-time occupation, and there can no more be part-time contemplatives than part-time Christians. Without the contemplative dimension in our lives, we cannot be fully human. This contemplative dimension is the fruit of our willingness to meet the discipline of learning to wait in silence and stillness, as well as the boredom and loneliness and sometimes the apparent emptiness which confront us in the waiting. Contemplation and action are both necessary to basic stability. There is a need to take regular times of quiet in order to be disciplined in the generous giving of self in our activity.

Interior peace is the fruit of Christ's overcoming and of the Holy Spirit's outpouring. This peace is the ground of Christian contemplation. T.S. Eliot's quest 'to apprehend the point of intersection of the timeless with time' is not a vague anticipation of the confrontation with God which will come to us all at the moment of death. Contemplation, in the Christian sense, is a living in the *now* of daily life in preparation for that moment of truth; it is a living in the realization of God's love and his claim upon us. Indeed, any experience of the reality of God rests upon the belief that we are able to love him because his love has created and redeemed us. For the Christian, the end of man is union with God in love, and we are meant to know something of that love in this present life. We are able to know it by prayer and contemplation and in loving relationship one with another in God. As St Paul tells us, we can know only in part, but we could know so much more than we do if we could face the cost of what a life lived in union with Christ demands; if we could open ourselves to the power of the Holy Spirit to enlarge and deepen those latent powers and potentialities that our human spirit possesses. After all, the Christian life is directed to a goal beyond all human expectation, a goal which can be attained only by strength far beyond our unaided human capacity. Therefore, contemplation is a gift to be received, to be prepared for, rather than something we can train ourselves to do. 'The Holy Spirit whom the Father will send in my name will teach you everything and will call to mind all that I have told you,' said Jesus. And St Paul said, 'Bear fruit in active goodness of every kind, and grow in the knowledge of God so that Christ may present us before himself as dedicated men.' Christian contemplation is incarnational, not a negative journey inwards, but the growth of unity of life and prayer, an increase in the knowledge of God shown forth by the wholeness of consecrated life.

Vacete et videte quoniam ego sum deus: 'Empty yourself

and know that I am God.' The Latin is so much stronger than the translation in the Authorized Version, 'Be still and know that I am God.' If we are truly empty, and then offer the ground of our soul and natural intelligence and faculties to wait upon God in the desire of love, we shall grow in the way of pure faith, hope and love, the way which is not dependent upon conscious realization and emotional experience. Christian prayer must never be seen as an escape from reality into a world of self-contemplation, but as receiving quietly and often covertly a knowledge of God wherein life becomes meaningful and unified. In Christian prayer the frequent sense of tension between contemplation and action is resolved, for both are recognized as aspects of the one great power of God's love poured into our hearts by the Holy Spirit, who is Love. There is thus a dividing line between the Christian and non-Christian way of life. Where all human beings must follow their reason and their conscience, informed by all the truth made available to them, the Christian must follow the way of God as revealed by Christ. This is the way of self-giving, death and resurrection. The Christian, united with Christ and empowered by the Holy Spirit, is able to obey completely the command to love God with the whole mind, the whole soul, the whole heart, the whole strength, and to love his neighbour as himself. In silence and contemplation the Christian opens himself to this unifying power of God. It is an openness to infused contemplation, a gift of God which he bestows when and to whom he wills. An undoubted truth about contemplative prayer upon which all masters of the spiritual life agree is that God gives his gifts when, where and how he chooses. He can as easily give the gift of contemplation to a busy housewife as to a cloistered nun. In contemplation God acts alone in absolute freedom. The awareness of contemplation may come suddenly in the midst of some other exercise of prayer, or even when the mind is occupied with other things. God takes over, as it were, and the experience of union with him that follows is wholly his operation. It may go as suddenly as it came, but the soul is left in no doubt that it has been visited by God and that the whole experience is God's act and nothing of its own endeavouring. The soul can no more command the presence of God than it can delay his withdrawal. It can only adore, and know itself to be a great sinner. The result of such visitations is a deeper penitence of the soul, a joyous rising up to accomplish God's will and a readiness to suffer for him. Progress in this contemplative way is best gauged by our willingness to suffer.

Another way of approaching the tension between prayer and action is to think in terms of leisure and work. To think of opportunities for leisure as opportunities for contemplation is to enrich the possibilities of ordinary Christian living. The Latin word *otium* means rest, peace or leisure, and its opposite is *negotium*, meaning business or work; St Bernard called the monastic life *negotissimum otium* – a very busy leisure. The Christian redeems work from being mere drudgery to make it something more enlarging and enriching. The picture given us in the Book of Genesis makes clear the ideal relationship between work and leisure, and Milton vivifies the Old Testament account. There is work in paradise, just as there is in our own daily life.

Now when as sacred light began to dawn
In Eden on the humid flow'rs that breathed
Their morning incense, when all things that breathe
From th'earth's great altar send up silent praise

To the Creator, and his nostrils fill
With grateful smell, forth came the human pair
And joined their vocal worship to the quire
Of creatures wanting voice; that done, partake
The season, prime for sweetest sense and airs;
Then commune how that day they best may ply
Their growing work; for much their work outgrew
The hands' dispatch of two gard'ning so wide.
And Eve first to her husband thus began:
   'Adam, well may we labour still to dress
This garden, still to tend to plant, herb and flow'r,
Our pleasant task enjoined, but till more hands
Aid us, the work under our labour grows,
Luxurious by restraint; what we by day
Lop overgrown, or prune, or prop or bind,
One night or two with wanton growth derides,
Tending to wild. Thou therefore now advise
Or hear what to my mind first thoughts present:
Let us divide our labours, thou where choice
Leads thee, or where most needs, whether to wind
The woodbine round this arbor, or direct
The clasping ivy where to climb, while I
In yonder spring of roses intermixed
With myrtle, find what to redress till noon.
For while so near each other thus all day
Our task we choose, what wonder if so near
Looks intervene and smiles, or object new
Casual discourse draw on, which intermits
Our day's work, brought to little, though begun
Early, and th'hour of supper comes unearned.'

John Milton, *Paradise Lost*, IX 192-225

Before the Fall, work is so joyful and rendered so wholly
to God that it is in itself leisure: after the Fall, however,

work becomes toilsome and servile. When work takes on the colour of toil, drudgery and servility it is the fruit of an unwilling obedience. It has no joy of co-operation with the will of God in it.

In opposition to the exclusive idea of work as activity, we must revive the idea of *otium* in its contemplative dimension. This is not incompatible with the heavy demands of daily work. Contemplative leisure must be an attitude of calm and silence. Leisure can become a form of the silence which is a pre-requisite of the apprehension of the real world. Only the silent hear. Contemplative leisure is a receptive attitude of mind which deepens the humility of the spirit and clears a path of descent into the mysterious nature of the world. It requires a very great degree of practice and patience through prayer to grow in this inward stillness. The way of the Desert Fathers was to leave the demands of social life and seek in their cells interior prayer, rest, peace, quiet, as well as the struggle of the interior conflict. A measure of this can be incorporated into every Christian life. The ability to sit still and listen is a positive and creative act, not a dead absence of activity. There is a story of St Anthony and the huntsman who reproved him for relaxing with his brethren outside his cell. St Antony told him to bend his bow and shoot one arrow after another, until at length the huntsman said: 'But if I keep my bow stretched always, it will snap'. Antony replied, 'It is the same for a monk'; and it is the same for any person.

The great Christian day of leisure is Sunday, and the event which has the capacity for holding work and leisure, contemplation and action in the most creative relation is the eucharist. The contemplative Christian must live eucharistically, for whenever he receives Holy Communion he offers himself, soul and body to be a lively sacrifice to God: and as he is united with Christ's offering to the Father in the power of the Holy Spirit, his whole personality, all that it is and does, must necessarily be involved in this offering. This is a valuable reminder of the priority of grace which comes to us as God's gift, something we can only accept. We take the sacrament in an action, but we receive it in contemplative humility by which we are ever disposed to receive in deeper measure. The contemplation of grace as we receive the sacrament insures against the dangers of preoccupation with self-realization, even though it be a refined and spiritual self.

It is perhaps relevant here to suggest that our recent renewal in liturgy in the West has tended to eliminate rather than emphasize the element of leisure for God. We have reduced our liturgical worship to bare structures which, however essential, have left us with a cerebral, concentrated 'work' liturgy. The Eastern liturgy has resisted this process. It contains repeated litanies and prayers said again and again, because cumulatively they express the resolution of contemplation and action which draws us nearer to God. G. K. Chesterton once compared this kind of leisured liturgy to a child playing with sand; you build him a castle and he knocks it down saying, 'Again, again!' This understanding of liturgy as a participation in an eternal dimension forbids clock-watching. When the deacon chants, 'Now it is time for God to act', space is made for our whole being to expand into an unselfconscious engagement in the fullness in which God created us. It is here that we practice the art and science of standing before God.

It is in eucharistic living that we attain creative leisure. The real cure of our misunderstanding of leisure as merely a break in work, or of silence as an escape from reality, is a renewed appreciation of all creation. The Paschal liturgy affirms in the words of the Book of Genesis, 'God saw all that he made, and behold, it was very good.' Leisure and silence should have the rhythmic repose of creative energy coming together in a contemplative unity. It can be likened to the ebb and flow of the waves of the sea, or, in liturgical worship, to the rhythmic pulse of the chant. Leisure and silence should have the dimension in which the spirit expands and is purified.

It is a growing knowledge of God by prayer that will lead us to recognize the true value and nature of silence. Prayer will deepen the interior stillness which relaxes tension and makes creative expression of leisure part of our total response to God. An element of silence in leisure will facilitate the discernment of what is good and profitable in the use of time given us, a discernment which is part of the gift of the Spirit. This use of silence in our lives is far from pointless and negative, far from harming others by coldness and self-absorption, far from self-centredness. The contemplative use of silence sees no ultimate good in itself. It is an instrument which points and leads beyond itself. John Donne described heaven as the place where there 'shall be no noise nor silence but one equal music'. Silence is a beginning, a way by which we learn the positive and difficult art of listening, of using not only our ears but our whole selves in order to attend.

CHAPTER THREE

The Path of Spiritual Progress

Silence prepares the way for the union of the soul with
the will of God and is an offering of perpetual rever-
ence to his majesty . . . it should be remembered that
silence must cover all the levels of the conscious life;
there must be an outward silence of speech and movement, a silence of the mind for the overcoming of vain
imagination and distractions, and a silence of the soul
in the surrender of the will to be still and know that
God is God, leading to a silence of spirit which is the
preparation for the fullness of contemplation.

The Rule of the Sisters of the Love of God

When one really loves, words become less important and
listening brings deeper awareness and greater sensitivity
to the meaning of love. It is what might be called a
listening prayer to which silence leads. Silence is the doorway through which we pass to a deeper understanding of
Christ's prayer for the world, and the deeper listening in
which it results marks the transition from the more active
forms of prayer, such as meditation, to a quieter and
more receptive contemplative prayer. In 1 Corinthians 2,
St Paul says, 'These are the things that God has revealed
to us through the Spirit, for the Spirit reaches the depths
of everything, even the depths of God.' In order for these
deep things to be heard, we need to be still and listen. A
relationship is stunted and sterile if one or other of the
participants keeps up a continuous monologue. As prayer

is a relationship with God, we need not be afraid of being silent; indeed, there must be a listening, attentive silence, or prayer time will become a sleep time! The real meaning of intercession is not telling God in one's own words of the needs and sorrows of the world, but through the silent attentive spirit focusing the love of God where the need is greatest.

On the path of spiritual progress we must not be afraid to feel within ourselves some of the violent passions and fears which we believe prayer can expose to Christ's reconciliation. As Christians we cannot escape the burden of sharing in the sorrows of mankind. This kind of prayer is both costly and a privilege, for as we learn to see our part in this burden of man's sin, something of the prayer of Christ is re-enacted in us. No matter how busy we are, we must not lose the dimension in daily life of being in Christ's prayer and reconciliation. Listening is a fundamental ingredient of this condition. In the rush of the world there is no small difficulty, when we stop talking, in retrieving the silence we have had necessarily to suspend. Our minds continue to work, and fasten on trivialities, our emotions rebel in some way or other, our wills struggle in the interests of self. These tensions must be overcome in order that we may truly hear. When we are not attentive listeners it is not only our own personal relationship with God that will be diminished, but even possibly the direct communication between God and another person. Our dissipation of mind, our instability and lack of courage to face ourselves, or to be vulnerable to others, frustrates God's intention that our prayer be a clear pathway to the discernment of the needs of each other.

The most difficult and decisive part of prayer is acquiring this ability to listen. Listening is no passive affair, a space when we happen not to be doing or speaking. Inactivity and superficial silence do not necessarily mean that we are in a position to listen. Listening is a conscious, willed action, requiring alertness and vigilance, by which our whole attention is focused and controlled. Listening is in this sense a difficult thing. And it is decisive because it is the beginning of our entry into a personal and unique relationship with God, in which we hear the call of our own special responsibilities for which God has intended us. Listening is the aspect of silence in which we receive the commission of God.

The obstacles to positive listening are numerous. Much of our time is spent talking and listening to ourselves. Our own voices are the chief obstacle to our listening either to God or to other people. We chatter away to others in attempts to make contact with them, to impress, amuse or instruct; sometimes we chatter even to relieve ourselves. We do an immense amount of talking in any ordinary day; not surprisingly, since speech is one of the chief means by which society functions. When we are not talking to others, we often talk to God in the imperative: 'Listen to me, God!' We then explain to him about ourselves, our neighbours, our needs, our hopes, our fears, bombarding him with information. Then follow our requests. And, of course, when we are talking neither to God nor to others we are probably carrying on a continuous dialogue with ourselves which goes on and on, blocking our ears to anything else, and allowing our conversation to monopolize our whole attention.

One moment of willed listening when we are alone, however, shows us how much we are missing, even of ordinary sounds. If we take our minds off ourselves for a moment, we may hear a bird singing, a bell in the distance, the gentle rustle of the wind in the leaves, the murmur of the tide as it ebbs and flows over the pebbles on the beach, even our own breathing. Generally, we drown such sounds with our interior chatter. It is not external noise but preoccupation with self which usually prevents us from listening. It is often said that our world is so full of noise that we can't listen any longer. Yet even when we do escape from the traffic, the jet planes, radio, television and all the ordinary noises of civilization, we still find it hard to listen. The external noises of the world are as nothing compared with the din we make within ourselves. We can be deaf to the loudest noise as long as our inner selves remain unstilled. Only later on do external noises become a distraction.

There is a whole asceticism of listening to be learned. It takes a conscious and controlled effort to become still and attentive, and to let others speak to us as themselves. It is the slow and exacting process of recalling our attention to the matter in hand, whether it be a person, a book, or perhaps the tools we handle. An aid towards accomplishing this art is to take a word or a phrase or a short passage from Scripture and give it our whole attention, resisting the desire to go on reading or to explore some related fact, but instead letting it speak to us until it begins to sing its own song within us. It is then that we are on the threshold of prayer, when our whole attention is caught and our whole being focused on God, with an awareness of immense need, or perhaps overwhelming delight.

T. S. Eliot was preoccupied with having the experience but missing the meaning. In order not to miss the meaning in verbal exchange we must empty ourselves of our preconceptions, prejudices and reservations, not only about the person to whom we are listening but also about the matter of which he or she may be talking. We shall do

35

this successfully only if we see listening to others as an extension and a fruit of our listening to God. In listening with this positive determination we make a space for God in our lives. It is by listening that we become aware of our own nothingness without God, and it is by listening with a growing sense of the coinherence of human lives that we avoid self-righteousness and are enabled to grow in compassion. Seen in this wider context, listening and silence can be equated with compassion and loving awareness of each other. We must beware of patronizing others, of any sense of conferring a benefit on them. Instead we must accept ourselves as very ineffectual human beings trying to respond in human terms to another human being, one who is no better nor worse, no more complicated, neither more nor less intelligent, sensitive and aware than ourselves. True listening obviously needs careful training. Silence and listening are not by themselves sufficient. When we have begun to learn to listen, we shall notice certain things. We shall actually begin to hear external sounds with our ears, and it is at this point that we can begin to discriminate and make ourselves choose what we will hear. This will lead us on to desire more and more external silence to correspond with the growing inner alertness and attentiveness which is the prelude to stillness before God. The solitary place, the lonely shore, these may have a real place in our prayer. We have to be able to hear external sounds before we can with any prudence choose among them and exclude those which are unnecessary. Then we shall notice that we have begun to listen to ourselves. More likely than not we shall dislike what we hear, but once we have begun to be still, once we have stopped deluding ourselves with our own ideas and suggestions, there is a chance that we may hear within ourselves what we most deeply desire but may still be afraid to face. Here again, we shall be in a position to exercise discernment about our inner promptings, and also to recognize how one way and another we may be tempted to use our activity as an escape route from that inner awareness which is God himself. And so we shall hear God. To speak of 'hearing' God is of course to use a metaphor. We are focusing our attention on God in order to hear what he is saying to us through the scriptures, liturgy, the circumstances of our lives, through other people. The Spirit broods over the waters of our chaos, and out of chaos he brings order.

Thus we hear others. There is a caveat to be entered on this subject, however. Precisely because of its importance, listening to others has become something of an idol among us, especially in these days of 'horizontal leadership'. We feel it imperative to listen to others, to hear what they are saying, and hear all of it. Psychology as well as religion urges us to do so. The humanities and the social sciences are as eager as theology to make us listen to others. Listening is indeed vital, but we must take care to remember that to understand is to *stand under the other*. Our missionary work is an example of where we have failed to do this; it has been the error of Christians in the past to be unprepared to listen to what the religions of the world have to say to us. In all our listening we must be mindful of two things. First, that it is not an easy matter for any of us to recognize our true identity. The search for our identity is lifelong, and we must therefore be attuned sensitively, and we must pray for discretion and patience as we listen to others. Together we have much more chance of making the discovery. And second, we must use discernment about that to which we listen. There is a great danger in opening ourselves to hear everything a person wants to say to us at that moment. Sometimes we genuinely cannot bear it, and it is the sin of curiosity that makes us listen to what we can neither understand nor share. Indeed, the persons concerned, having told all, will almost inevitably at a later date regret having done so, because we were inadequate, or because they think we have betrayed them, or because they are frightened or feel ashamed. It is not always necessary to hear everything. There is a limit to how much we can profitably hear from the lips of another person on any single occasion.

Though speech is the most obvious means of communication we have, it is silence and listening which do more than anything to unite us with God and with each other. It is not our activity which blocks the lines of communication between ourselves and God, and between ourselves and those around us, but our egoism. Listening silence can be a means of purification. Only a listening silence can lead to a stilling of the mind, a cessation of the chatter surging up from the unconscious. The cleansing of memory is that aspect of purgation which makes space for the work of listening, which is our part in the dialogue of prayer with God. There is no point in trying to beat the mind into a shape of concentration: that is an effort of will very different from waiting on the power of God to draw all our faculties into unity. It is the uprising of love in the heart, the desire to belong utterly to God that cleanses us, and during this process it is for God to deal with the stirrings of our natural being. It is only when a soul is wholly given to Christ to be formed in charity that there is a complete quieting of self. Only in the willingness to listen in silence can God's will be heard.

All that has so far been said can be found exemplified and focused in the lives of the two remarkable Carmelite saints, St Teresa of Avila and St John of the Cross. In the lives of both, the dichotomy of prayer and action was resolved by their wholehearted giving of self to God. The life of action and the experience of prayer become the one expression of a total commitment to love. St Teresa constantly reminded her nuns that spiritual progress was not like walking along a straight road. To use her own simile, it is like the development of the butterfly, each stage quite different from the previous one. The butterly lays an egg; the egg hatches into a caterpillar. At this stage of its life the insect feeds, during which period the caterpillar grows, though its skin does not. Therefore the caterpillar sheds its skin two or three times. It then pupates and becomes a chrysalis, winding itself into a silk cocoon and appearing quite dead. Yet inside, though there is no apparent life, there takes place unseen the most significant change of all. When the cocoon splits open at last, out comes not a caterpillar but a butterfly with large, bright-coloured wings. It dries itself in the summer sunshine and proceeds to lay eggs from which the next generation will hatch. This analogy could, of course, be carried too far, but from it we can at least see that there are in this life constant permutations of the soul's development. We cannot say that at any one moment we have moved out of the purgative way into fuller union, nor can we believe that there will be no need to retrace our steps to those fundamental dispositions of the soul such as penitence and humility which are the foundation stones for all true ascent of the mount of prayer.

Both Teresa and John of the Cross are examples of the true tradition that visions and other psychological phenomena are not necessarily manifestations of the Holy Spirit or even a direct preparation for such, but something which our bodily and psychic nature may have to endure in the growing process of our unification. Both these saints emphasize that sanctity, properly speaking, is not connected with extraordinary phenomena. Teresa herself says:

> The highest perfection consists not in interior favours, or in great raptures or visions, or in the spirit of prophecy but the bringing of our wills so closely into conformity with the will of God that as soon as we realize that he wills anything, we also desire it ourselves with all our might, and take the bitter with the sweet, knowing that to be his Majesty's will.
>
> St Teresa of Avila,
> *Foundations*, ch. 5

This underscores Teresa's definition of sanctity in *The Interior Castle* where she emphasizes the complete conformity with the will of God which is the whole aim of those who would truly pray. Readers of the works of Teresa are often surprised and at first put off at finding how little teaching there is on what to do in prayer, or how the time of prayer should actually be spent. Her attitude is clear, however. Teresa leaves her nuns in no doubt that it is impossible to see prayer in isolation from the whole context of Christian living. What happens in prayer depends upon and is necessarily integrated with what we do with the rest of our time. Hence her insistence on love, humility and obedience as the necessary accompaniment to all prayer at every stage. She has much to teach us. The modern mind may not find it easy to digest her rather lengthy and often diffuse sentences, but her teaching is worth the exploration.

The child Teresa left her home with her brother to seek martyrdom but was brought quickly back. The nun in her late sixties, worn out by her constant work for the Church, truly lived a life of martyrdom by bringing others to the realization of God. So for Christians today the call is the same. We are all called to stand, wherever we may be, as fortresses in the darkness, in the night of the Church as we know it and as it has for centuries been known, to stand in the day of martyrdom, whether of blood or of mind, unconquerable in our dependence on God. God calls us to nothing less than to stand unshakeable as the shakeable is being shaken. This is a call to all Christians to be men and women of prayer, that they may speak out of personal knowledge and experience of the things of God to those who are seeking reality. The greatest contribution of Teresa was to show that the path of spiritual progress is essentially ordinary. It is not outside the path of normality, but in it. It is simply a case of natural growth in what God intends for us all, requiring the immediate contact with him which is the listening responsiveness of contemplative prayer.

Some people have a resistance to St John of the Cross and his so-called systematized methods of prayer in which he sets out the dark nights of the senses and the spirit as the necessary preparation for a personal living experience of the union of love between God and the soul. In fact this darkness, alternating with light, is part of all human experience of prayer. The nights of which John of the Cross speaks apply not just to experience in prayer but also to the costly demands of the Christian way of life and give us a guide line by which to meet and to respond to the challenge of the way of the cross. On a practical level John of the Cross learnt this at the hands of his brethren, not only during his years of incarceration but also at the end of his life when he was virtually rejected by his order. All of us at some point in our prayer or in our daily life reach a point which is a kind of death, but the great men and women of the Christian faith, like John of the Cross and Teresa of Avila, are living examples that it is at the point of nothingness that our emptiness will be filled with a new presence and power. A new circuit of love will begin, if we remember always that it can be but a foretaste of what is to come, provided that in daily life we are prepared to listen more and more closely to the voice of God. The lesson we have to learn has an identical method and result: to listen to God alone, and to listen to him for his own sake, and not for anything we might want to hear. St John of the Cross writes:

> The desire of the soul is not always supernatural, but only when God infuses it, and himself gives it strength, and then it is a very different thing from natural desire, and, until God infuses it, it has little or no merit. When you of your own accord, would fain desire God, this is no more than a natural desire; nor will it be anything more, until God be pleased to inform it supernaturally. And thus when you, of your own accord, would fain attach your desires to spiritual things, and when you would lay hold upon the pleasure of them, you exercise your own natural desire, and are spreading a cataract over your eye and are an animal being. And you cannot therefore understand or judge of that which is spiritual, which is higher than any natural desire and sense.
>
> St John of the Cross,
> *Living Flame of Love*, 3:75

Here the metaphor of sight replaces that of hearing. Yet, St John would say, when our sight is distorted, so too is our ability to listen at the deep level which is the fruit of Godward action and contemplation. Elsewhere, St John of the Cross gives us an indication of the depth to which the truly Christian ear can listen:

Of peace and piety interwound
This perfect science had been wrought,
Within the solitude profound
A straight and narrow path is taught,
Such secret wisdom there I found
That there I stammered, saying naught,
Transcended knowledge with my thought.

St John of the Cross,
Verses written after an ecstasy, St 3

CHAPTER FOUR

The Apostolate of Prayer

This age which by its very nature is a time of crisis, of revolution and of struggle, calls for the special searching and questioning which is the work of the Christian in silence, his meditation, his prayer; for he who prays searches not only in his own heart but he plunges deep into the heart of the whole world in order to listen more intently to the deepest and most neglected voices that proceed from its inner depths.

Thomas Merton, *The Climate of Monastic Prayer*

We must learn to listen and be still with our whole attention, but this is not an end, any more than silence is an end in itself. Consider the supreme mystery of the silence of Mary before the coming of the incarnate Son. At the Annunciation we see a woman who listened totally with her whole self, but that was not the end. Out of that listening she not only heard the call, she obeyed. God's word spoke itself fully in her silence. There is also the silence of Mary at the foot of the cross. She was able to add nothing to the suffering of her Son, but by her silent compassion and identification with his will, she is for eternity the perfect example of the human will uniting itself with the supreme offering of God's redemptive action. Here listening and action reach a climax. The one who truly listens is also the one who truly obeys. If we accept the call to still ourselves in order to listen to God, we may be required to take action, and the result may be as devastating as it was for Mary, who gave birth to a Son who she knew would bear the suffering of the world.

Prayer is a way of encounter. This is the Christian way. Man becomes fully himself through the adjustment of his relationship with those realities other than himself amongst whom or in which his life is lived. He must face them, and relate himself freely to them. The quiet contemplative dimension of faith is not a vocal dialogue with God, but a deeper knowledge that prayer leads us into a state of 'being', a stage of prayer that has superseded the use of our mental activity in which it was we who were doing the praying. Our prayer life has now moved into that stage of greater communication where there is an experience of the presence of God acting not through any sense of consolation, but through the whole of his being, which cannot be reduced to any idea or concept. In all things we are in Christ in his offering to the Father by the power of the Holy Spirit. Prayer descends through silence and a deeper listening to the cost of Calvary. The answer to evil is the bringing of the triumph of Calvary into the world. It is those who hear the call of God and obey who stand firm in the spiritual conflict; those who are empty of self, entirely dependent on God in simplicity, recognizing their sinfulness, knowing that they can do nothing of themselves but only as God works in them. If, in bringing our prayerfulness into the action of the world the way is hard, it is only that the surrender may be more complete. This unity of contemplation and action is Christ's call to all of us to partake in his reconciliation of the world. The common vocation of all the baptized is to respond to the needs of the world. For this we are given the means of our particular vocations, the priesthood, the active life, the married life, the enclosed life, the solitary life. We are given both the place and the people to form and fashion us for the unique place and function which each of us has in the whole Christ. The deeper listening of prayer gives the discernment of recognition of the role to which God is calling us for the purposes of reconciliation in the world. That is the ultimate meaning of vocation, and that is the only true end.

Christians must learn and re-learn the lesson of saying 'Not I, but Christ'. To hear the summons of God pre-requires an unconditional loyalty to Christ alone. The dual note in Christianity of worldliness and unworldliness is part of man's duality, belonging to him as a creature of God made in God's image. The contemplative element in the life of any Christian must be apostolic in the simplicity by which it proclaims the teaching of the Gospel. If the active apostolate does not proceed from the apostle's own union with God, there can be no enduring vitality in the Christian life of action: the measure of apostolic witness is not to be sought in the amount of active work accomplished, but in the purity of faith and love expressed in the genuine simplicity of a truly humble life, open and obedient to God.

This is the true relevance of all religious life. A community, or parish or family, whatever form its ministry takes, by reason of its prayer, its sanctity and its adherence to the Gospel, shows that the meaning of its life is the depth of encounter, with self, with others and ultimately with God. This is the power by which the Gospel is communicated and is the spiritual impact which people recognize as real. Psychiatry is constantly telling us how much mental illness is caused because people are starved inwardly while society presses them to put all their energies and interests into their external work. The essential witness of the apostolic life is the life of union with God and the spirit of self-discipline and self-denial expressed both corporately and in the life of each individual member of the community of the Church. Genuine contemplative prayer which has listened and heard and responded from the depths is never unworldly in a cold and sterile way, but of the world in its Christ-like selflessness and purity of heart which gathers up the sins and conflicts of the world and baptizes them with tears of concern and re-pentance. No form of the prayerful life properly and honestly lived can be confused with escapism, a negative flight from reality: that would be a travesty of the truth. The response of the early monks and solitaries who made a city of the wilderness was rooted in a stark realism of faith in God and an acceptance of the battle of the spirit. The Christian life which is founded upon a belief in and experience of prayer as encounter, understands how facile is the notion that God manifests himself only in progress, in the improvement of standards of living, in the spread of medicine and the reform of abuses in organized religion: real spiritual progress can be achieved only through catastrophe and suffering, the encounter of new levels and new depths after the purgation which accom-panies major upheavals. Every such period of agony clears away the old to make a space for the new dimension of a deeper spiritual insight.

It is with these deeper spiritual insights that contem-plation and action should alike be concerned. Within the silence and the measure of retreat available to all, within the discipline of family, community and parish life, given in all its vigour to God, there must be a listening and attentiveness to God in which the suffering and doubt of humanity are heard more clearly than in the hurly-burly of immediate involvement. In prayer the things of the world are seen in a truer perspective and proportion, because they are seen in the light of God's purpose. The Christian life stands for eternalism and not conservatism, and demands a constant chastening of our methods and our structures by which we strive to carry out God's commission: there is no substitute for the flexibility and simplicity of biblical witness. It is the perfect balance of contemplation and action which characterizes the prophets and makes the genuine apostle.

We are, it is generally recognized, living in a time of recovery, when the spiritual riches of the West and of the Orthodox East are once more being brought more closely together for the benefit of our own tradition, so that we may interpret more effectively to the great non-Christian religions of the East the mystery of the fullness of Christ. In post-Reformation times, the West, whether Catholic or Protestant, tended to look upon contemplation and the contemplative way as being only for the few. Very often the principles of contemplation have been regarded as ecstatic and dangerous. Only quite recently have we in the West begun to realize again the truth that the Orthodox East has never lost: that the normal development of prayer takes root in the context of silence and listening, and flowers in the action of reconciliation in the world, the apostolate of prayer.

The apostolate of prayer is a rhythm of sacrificial love, taking its pattern from the Trinity. The Son goes from and returns to the Father: he is sent by the Father and he sends the disciples; the Son is loved by the Father and he loves his disciples, and the disciples must love one another. The Father and the Son are one, and so too must the disciples be one. And the Spirit of Truth, the Advocate— he too is sent. Jesus goes and the Spirit comes. Jesus goes so that the Spirit may be sent. Father, Son, Spirit and disciples are caught up in an exchange of sacrificial love. This is what being sent means in the Christian life. The one who is being sent, the apostle, is not sent to carry out a task, and then report back. He is sent to share, communicate the good news, but above all he is sent to give himself, just as the Son was sent by the Father to give himself for the life of the world. The apostle is the one who is sent to be spent. Thus, when we talk about apostles, the apostolic nature of the Church, and the apostolate of prayer, we are not talking about a pipeline, or a relay race, but about a universal dance in which mankind is being taken up into a sending and being sent, into the sacrificial love which is the life of the triune God. The apostles, and those who are called to share their ministry are, as Austin Farrer put it, 'walking sacraments' of the truth. They sacramentally represent and enact the divine receiving and sending and being sent to which all Christians are called. As 'walking sacraments' we are called and drawn by love to share in Christ's mysterious work of atonement and reconciliation, by which he breaks down all the barriers between man and God, by which he takes away the Sin of the world, all that separates us from God; the mysterious work of Christ, focused on the hill of Calvary, of which his whole life of obedience and offering was an integral part, the redemptive way through death into the fullness of his Father's kingdom. Life, death, resurrection and ascension: it is by his total action from the first moment of his incarnation to the entrance into the heavenly places, by the whole sweep of Christ's redeeming work, that we are reconciled to the Father.

The pattern of the Trinity demonstrates to us that it is not so much the action itself which is important, as the love in us that leads to the action. The fruit of the response to the call heard and obeyed, which is the apostolate of prayer, is the love of Christ shown forth amongst the brethren. The love of God flows in contemplation, and the love of Christ flows out, consuming the apostle with its fire, and overflowing in sacrificial work and offering. When we reach the stage of apostleship, we see that prayer cannot be merely a matter of personal communion with God alone. Once the knowledge that we are being drawn into the reconciling love of God has touched our hearts, however dimly, there must be the desire to be drawn more deeply into the meaning of his redemptive love for mankind.

The movement of man towards reconciliation springs out of the love of God, born of the deep contemplation of his nature. When a man is possessed by the love of God, he must respond and long for others to respond to his love from which is derived the impetus and courage to give ourselves generously to the work of intercession. As we allow ourselves to become possessed by God, we must expect to experience the pain of the world's lack of love for God and of man's cruelty to his fellow men. This gives to prayer its twofold action in the one movement of reconciliation: the Godward action of loving adoration and penitence for sin in ourselves and in others, and a deep sense of participation in the world's anguish because of the close-knit co-inherence of mankind. The first is figured in the vertical beam of the cross, pointing Godwards, and the second by the horizontal beam, embracing the continuity of all human experience. We cannot escape the responsibility of a world torn by war, by racial disunity, abject poverty in the midst of plenty, and all other sin which corrupts society.

Therefore, in prayer we must begin with ourselves, in the selfless sense, and our own sin, because the seeds of the world's greatest evil are in each one of us. The selfishness which we rightly condemn as it manifests itself in others, we must admit to find lurking in our own hearts. For all of us the quest and the demand for purity of heart is paramount, for no prayer can claim to be part of Christ's reconciliation unless it purges out the hidden falsity which lies in all of us. The process of the stripping away of all that is unreal, untrue, is an essential part of the prayer of reconciliation. Only the pure vessel can be a channel of God's redeeming love to the world: only the pure heart and will in conformity with the will of God can effectively intercede on behalf of sinners or be part of the identification with Christ's prayer and offering which alone give value to anything we do.

To participate in Christ's reconciliation means to open the whole being to God in the circumstances to which he has called us. It is through the stripping of self, through the order and discipline of life, that we shall grow to show forth the fruits of Christ's victory over sin and death. This is the true end of Christian asceticism, and it is the positive proof that our prayer and life are being simplified, purified and united with Christ's prayer. St Teresa, in *The Way of Perfection*, indicates that God does not force our wills as we establish the form of apostolic prayer: rather than compel our will, God prefers to face the risk of a part failure in his design. Love draws out, it does not compel, and God's love is given, not sold.

Suffering in itself is worth nothing. Only love can give life. Jesus Christ forged out of suffering and death the material of redemption, and so the redemption which has been lived and perfectly offered by Jesus, the head of the body of humanity, must now be realized day by day in the members of the body. This is the way for all Christians, and our prayer must be strong enough to take the same way of the cross. There is therefore no separation between the apostolate of prayer and action. They are two aspects of a harmonious whole, two manifestations of a God-centred life. Each must be activated by the Holy Spirit. When we have learned to remain constantly in the presence of God we become apostles filled with a consuming zeal that all men should know and be drawn by the love of God. Then we shall be able to echo the words of the prophet Elijah which became the two-fold motto of the Teresian Carmel: 'The Lord liveth in whose sight I stand,' and, 'With zeal have I been zealous for the Lord God of hosts.' Action and prayer are different modes of expressing the same truth. The way of prayer is not a subtle escape from the Christian dimension of the incarnation and redemption. It is a way of following Christ, of sharing in his passion and resurrection, of being part of his mediatorial prayer. The apostles went forth to turn the world upside down, strengthened and purified not only by the outpouring of the Holy Spirit but also by their participation in the Lord's passion and resurrection. 'All authority in heaven and earth has been given to me,' said the risen Christ:

> Go therefore, make disciples of all the nations; baptize them in the name of the Father and of the Son and of the Holy Spirit, and teach them to observe all the commands I gave you. And know that I am with you always; yes, to the end of time.
>
> Matthew 28:19-20 (J.B.)

That compassion is a personal challenge to all of us, and it should engender in us confidence and hope, and enable us to balance prayer and activity in due proportion. It is by the depth of our prayer that the charismatic power of the Holy Spirit operates as truly today as after Pentecost.

The infused love of contemplation is the release of the love of God, and that love is inseparable from its demonstration towards others. The love of God and the love of man merge.

The eucharist captivates the essence of the apostolate of prayer. All Christian prayer is being gathered up into Christ's thanksgiving that the Father has given him power in the Holy Spirit to draw all things into the one unity of love. Participation in the eucharist is a participation in the rhythm of love and unity within the life of the Trinity, and it is the source and motive of all true apostolic work. The work of God is achieved through no technique of human wisdom, but through oblation of the self. We are only channels through which the love and compassion of redemption may flow. This is portrayed in the Book of Revelation through the simile of the incense: the incense of our offering, our prayer, is carried up to heaven as part of the offering of Christ, the eternal High Priest. Unless the incense is burnt, the smoke cannot ascend. The charcoal must first be well lighted, and we must make a space in our lives for the cleansing fire of purgation and purification if the smoke of the incense of our prayer is to ascend right into the courts of God. To complete the simile, it is because it is fully consumed in the fire that the incense is fully offered. Chapter 7 of the Book of Revelation tells us that there are countless

people who have been through the great persecution, and because they have washed their robes white again in the blood of the Lamb, they now stand in front of God's throne and serve him day and night in his sanctuary . . . They will never hunger or thirst again . . . because the Lamb who is at the throne will be their

shepherd and will lead them to springs of living water
. . .

Rev. 7:14-17 (J.B.)

There are still those today who experience the martyrdom of blood, but it should not be forgotten that there is also the white martyrdom of those who are prepared to give themselves to the purifying fire of divine love in sharing in the work of prayer and the mediation of the Son of God. By reason of our baptism we are all committed to one aspect or another of this form of martyrdom. The Church today is full of schemes for reform, of returning to this or that idea of relevant expansion and expression of the Gospel. All such things have their due place, but the power of prayer is essential to mission and renewal. If we give ourselves to prayer, God's love and power will not be denied us in our activity. Those who suffer pain for the sake of Christ and for the redeeming of the world's sin re-enact on a small scale in their own lives the re-demptive action of God himself. There is no other answer to the problem of pain and suffering in the world. The basis of our Christian witness and mission is by prayer and faith to apply in our daily lives the fact that suffering, pain and difficulty, accepted positively and offered sac-rificially in love, unite us deeply with Christ's passion and resurrection, from which the transforming power of di-vine love is released to heal the wounds and deformities of ourselves and the world. This occurs not only in the extraordinary occasions of pain and difficulty that may come to us from time to time, but also in those unme-morable events of daily life: weariness of mind and body, the constant ringing of the telephone, the knock on the door, the personal slight or sense of injustice, some frus-tration of our plans. These are the raw material of the

54

sacrificial fire of our daily offering. Their acceptance and use determines whether our fire burns brightly or merely smoulders, whether it gives forth much or little heat and light for the furthering of God's kingdom and his glory.

Christ always lives to make intercession in us. Intercession is an indispensable aspect of the apostolate of prayer, and the great awesome challenge of it is that it is the point of prayer at which we shall stand with Christ in tension: it is there that the reconciling love and power of God meets the pain and suffering of the world, of individuals and of ourselves. It is at this point that we are ourselves most vulnerable. Interceding is not reminding God of his duties, it is taking a step towards the heart of the world. We proclaim the victory of the cross, and by prayer in union with Christ's redemptive love we are brought to be channels of his love, to bring joy where there is sorrow, life where there is death, unity where God's unity for mankind has been splintered and shattered in a thousand different ways. This kind of prayer requires a close union with God and with our fellow men who are united to us in the body of Christ. We must never in any way try to manipulate God's purposes for those for whom we pray but, giving ourselves unconditionally to God, be instruments to be used as he wills, making a space in which divine love can surround the person for whom we pray and in which the healing, creative side of the love of God can work for a man's greater wholeness and sanctification. This is how the whole body of Christ is built up.

Christians, whatever place they occupy in the Church, are basically human, with problems as well as potential, but it is more than a human response that God asks of us, in the sense that we can never respond to the needs of others entirely in our own resources. It is through the

55

indwelling of Christ in our hearts, the contemplative path to action, that our human response is made in co-operation with God himself. We cannot *do* Christianity, we can *be* Christians, and it is from our individual relationships with God that our doing should arise. It is the enabling power of the Holy Spirit which draws from our human raw material the apostolic response:

> I thank Jesus Christ our Lord, who has given me strength, and who judged me faithful enough to call me into his service, even though I used to be a blasphemer and did all I could to injure and discredit the faith.
>
> 1 Timothy 1:12 (J.B.)

God has accepted us with all our shortcomings, and we must therefore accept ourselves in the same image. The apostle in prayer can never pretend to be other than he is, and he can have no recourse to the deceitful comfort of a success image so easily adopted to avoid criticism and to protect from exposure. The relationship with God in prayer, which is the engagement in *being* a Christian, involves an ultimate choice which must be made alone with God, face to face with him, at the very depths of encounter. It means the gift of ourselves in true love, requiring a gift of courage. It is more difficult to be loved than to be a lover, because in allowing ourselves to be loved we must be what we are. Being ourselves, therefore, leads us to being Christians:

> Mercy, however, was shown me, because until I became a believer I had been acting in ignorance; and the grace of our Lord filled me with faith and with the love that is in Jesus Christ.
>
> 1 Timothy 1:13–14 (J.B.)

If we have not accepted our weaknesses, our lives will be something of a charade, but if we have accepted them, we can bring them to Christ. The apostolate of prayer requires response to the challenges of the Gospel. Things do not remain as they were once the light of the Gospel has been shed upon them. The Gospel is meant always to challenge. The message of John the Baptist reminds us that we are called to an apostolate of repentance: there is to be a movement of the heart, a movement of the spirit, a movement towards God which is more than any change of order. It is something which involves a complete redirection of our lives, accepting the will and the purposes of God in every aspect of our lives. Paul invokes woe on him who does not preach the Gospel. We must all as apostles of Christ preach the Gospel in our own human way filled with the love of Christ, proclaiming the fact of a new living relationship. We are the sons and daughters of God.

Joy must always be the note of our loving response to God. We should be careful, however, that we do not manufacture it. Christian joy is not just human brightness and cheerfulness. Sometimes such brightness and cheerfulness can be very depressing! We must bring to our apostolate the depth of joy that cannot be manufactured or conjured up, but which comes as the gift of God, something which must be sought always not as an acquisition, but as the fruit of the opening of the heart to God himself. The Christian moves in a reality in which weaknesses are made perfect in strength, with sorrow in which he can always rejoice, provided he is prepared to pay the cost. This joy is the fullness of God himself. It is a fullness we cannot understand merely by the exercise of the intellect: we cannot understand as finite creatures, brought into existence by God's love and power, how we are able to attain the fullness of being which is the fullness of God himself. We are to be strong to grasp with all God's people the breadth, length and height of the love of Christ, and to know it, *though it is beyond our knowledge*. We are to set ourselves to the task of knowing what is beyond knowledge, and so to enter more deeply into the relationship which God wills for us, that we may attain to fullness of being. We must seek to know God's love, knowing that it is beyond knowledge, because love is not the product of mankind. It is not something tangible like the objects which surround us.

We shall strive to know God who is love, and the love we are striving to know is God himself. We can therefore know and not know. We may know one another and rightly believe it, but we can never exhaust the knowledge of one another. So with God. We are to seek to know all the great riches of the love of Christ, knowing that while we can know, we can never know all. For God is love, God is infinite, and his universal purpose is something which embraces us, draws us to him that we may know that this life is a relationship with love inexhaustible. That is the great joy of Christianity, the great joy of being called to a particular relationship with God. It is the infinite God with his infinite love who pours himself into us so that we can speak of Christ dwelling in us to those in the cause of whom we are made apostles. Through the apostolate of prayer we must make ourselves available to God and to each other, so that the channels of the work of God remain viable and spontaneous. The apostolate of prayer requires the maturity to be accessible while still preserving the time and space for the contemplative wholeness and peacefulness of prayer which enable the Christian to communicate the reconciling calm of God through what he is. This balance between prayer and action will give to the apostolate of each of us the integrity which stamped so unmistakably the ministry of Christ himself:

Go forth, therefore, and make all nations my disciples; baptize them in the name of the Father and the Son and the Holy Spirit, and teach them to observe all that I have commanded you. And be assured, I am with you always, to the end of time.

Matthew 28:19–20 (N.E.B.)

Contemplative action informs a true spirit of service. A memorable icon of the humility of service is Christ washing the feet of the disciples.

During supper, Jesus, well aware that the Father had entrusted everything to him, and that he had come from God and was going back to God, rose from table, laid aside his garments and, taking a towel, tied it round him. Then he poured water into a basin, and began to wash his disciples' feet and to wipe them with a towel.

When it was Simon Peter's turn, Peter said to him, 'You, Lord, washing my feet?' Jesus replied, 'You do not understand now what I am doing, but one day you will.' Peter said, 'I will never let you wash my feet.' 'If I do not wash you,' Jesus replied, 'you are not in fellowship with me.' 'Then, Lord,' said Simon Peter, 'not my feet only: wash my hands and head as well!'

Jesus said, 'A man who has bathed needs no further washing; he is altogether clean; and you are clean, though not every one of you.' He added the words 'not every one of you' because he knew who was going to betray him.

After washing their feet and taking his garments

again, he sat down. 'Do you understand what I have done for you?' he asked. 'You call me "Master" and "Lord", and rightly so, for that is what I am. Then if I, your Lord and Master, have washed your feet, you also ought to wash one another's feet. I have set you an example: you are to do as I have done for you. In very truth I tell you, a servant is not greater than his master, nor a messenger than the one who sent him. If you know this, happy are you if you act upon it.'

John 13:3–17 (N.E.B.)

The quality of apostolic service is to have a sense of the infinite value of each individual, of the great flood of love that God has for his people, a love far exceeding the love that any of us can show in the apostolate of service. Charity should rule the life of the Christian and of the whole Church, whether it be in the parish, prison, university or factory. Christians are in the spirit of service called to leadership, and the bond that holds the members and the leaders together should be a fruit of the Holy Spirit present with them. It is in this concept of the servant that unity is most truly established. It needs as much humility and love to receive as to give and so in the apostolate of service, which is a fruit of the apostolate of prayer, there must be a mutuality of giving and receiving. An aspect of the role of the serving Christian is a readiness to be served by others. The Christian must discern in prayer the gifts and expertise of those around him, and allow them to use their gifts without giving way to a sense of inferiority or jealousy. This kind of mutuality is very difficult to achieve, and will be attained only through facing the problems inevitably present and praying for the welding power of the love of God himself.

Service presupposes suffering. As Jesus at the Last

Supper and on Calvary was the living bread which was taken, blessed, broken and distributed so that in him all might be offered in his prayer and sacrifice for mankind, so in the carrying out of his apostolate the Christian must be ready to be taken, broken, offered and distributed. This can be lived out in Christ only in proportion as the Christian knows himself to be the least of the brethren. Those nearest to Christ know as his mother knew that a sword must pierce their own hearts as it did hers, and that at the peak of loving service they can only stand, as Mary did, at the foot of the cross contemplating and hearing the will of God. Just as it is the one who loves most who is supremely the servant, so it was the sinner whose only claim was that she loved much, who in St Luke's Gospel claimed the unique privilege of the washing of feet with tears.

One of the Pharisees invited him to eat with them; he went to the Pharisee's house and took his place at table. A woman who was living an immoral life in the town had learned that Jesus was at table in the Pharisee's house and had brought oil of myrrh in a small flask. She took her place behind him, by his feet, weeping. His feet were wetted with her tears and she wiped them with her hair, kissing them and anointing them with the myrrh. When his host the Pharisee saw this he said to himself, 'If this fellow were a real prophet, he would know who this woman is that touches him, and what sort of woman she is, a sinner.' Jesus took him up and said, 'Simon, I have something to say to you.' 'Speak on, Master,' said he. 'Two men were in debt to a money-lender: one owed him five hundred silver pieces, the other fifty. As neither had anything to pay with, he let them both off. Now which will love him most?' Simon replied, 'I should think the one that was let off most.' 'You are right,' said Jesus. Then turning to the woman, he said to Simon, 'You see this woman? I came to your house: you provided no water for my feet; but this woman has made my feet wet with her tears and wiped them with her hair. You gave me no kiss; but she has been kissing my feet ever since I came in. You did not anoint my head with oil; but she has anointed my feet with myrrh. And so, I tell you, her great love proves that her many sins have been forgiven; where little has been forgiven, little love is shown.' Then he said to her, 'Your sins are forgiven.' The other guests began to ask themselves, 'Who is this, that he can forgive sins?' But he said to the woman, 'Your faith has saved you; go in peace.'

Luke 7:36–50 (N.E.B.)

God's call is to radical service. At the moment when we finally see him face to face, Christ will not ask us whether or not we have supported the established order of things, worn ourselves out with activities, kept the hierarchical structures intact, pleased everybody. His question will be that of Jesus to Simon Peter on the day of his resurrection, whether or not we have loved Christ and fed his flock. Jesus in his dealings with the apostles was always trying to widen their spiritual understanding and lead them away from their concern with their own material welfare to an increased love of God and man. Similarly, the more a Christian keeps his own inner life God-orientated, the more he will realize that men have a desire to grow up in Christ and a real longing for God. So he will try to see what God is doing in others, keeping close behind the Holy Spirit, who is the true director of souls. The apostolate of prayer requires steadfastness in prayer to God and in the mutuality of loving service. The honesty of mutuality will not allow the Christian to gloss over the great problems of the world. People will ask him how God can be a God of love if he allows so much universal pain and suffering, especially the undeserved suffering of the poor and needy, the young and defenceless, the aged and unwanted. The Church, in its constitution not as the organized institution but as the body of ordinary men and women who are searching for an answer to their suffering, doubts and fears, will find in the apostle of prayer, precisely because he has shared in their suffering, a living proclamation that Jesus Christ is himself the good news communicated through the apostle as an instrument of God; the human instrument who is being rather than doing Christianity. The apostle in prayer will have the authentic note in which God himself is instantly recognizable.

Diligence in the reading of scripture and other studies which will challenge an interpretation of the Gospel message is indispensable in reconciling a largely unbelieving world. The apostolate of prayer cannot be content in supporting the faithful remnant who attend church services, though they indeed must be part of the work of reconciliation. The true apostle has no smaller field of responsibility than the world. The more a Christian carries out on his knees the commission of God to serve all men with whom he comes into contact, the more he will be convinced of the necessity to pray; praying not only at those times when he is in the context of Church, but also when he is laid out before the Lord to be still, to listen in order to know more deeply what gift of himself God is waiting to give him, and what the nature of his response should be to this invitation of love. Worship and prayer are the tools in trade of religious and priests, yet the laity have often gone deeper into the search of informal prayer than the clergy, and the laity are sometimes down-hearted when they find so little encouragement given to them in their prayer life. Lay Christians have in general been more quick than priests to realize that in the age of flux and tensions in which we live prayer itself has not escaped the turmoil: with changing theology we are led again and again into a new and developing relationship with God who is the primary partner in prayer. This is precisely why we must take prayer so seriously, for the gift of the Spirit is given for growth and not for stagnation. In order to fan into flame the gift which God has given us, we must be nourished by an ever deepening inwardness. The disciplines of silence, times of withdrawal, prayer and study ensure against destruction by an immoderate self-sacrificing activism which may lead to personal laxity and in the end to an overdrawing on spiritual reserves. And it is necessary to be aware of the danger of too much thinking about God, rather than relaxing in his presence and waiting upon him in emptiness. The man of prayer must first learn to make his relationship with God mean-ingful and authentic for himself so that he can be enabled by the power of the Holy Spirit to help others to authen-ticate the knowledge of God for themselves. So the Chris-tian has the dual responsibility to make time for his own encounter with God and to be accessible to others as a conveyor of the Gospel. This is what the people of God look for, and they should not go away unnourished.

Calvary from one viewpoint is an example of the world's greatest failure, and the vocation of those who follow in the footsteps of the Master might be classified from a worldly standpoint as a divine folly, as indeed could the life of the monk or nun. We must be prepared for this, while remembering that it was the joy of the divine folly which the first Christians so gallantly typified. The participation of Christ's offering of reconciliation and his renewal and healing of man's deepest need must be re-enacted and seen to be accepted and joyfully embraced by all Christians in their various ministries. The Christian is called to give praise to God, to tend the anguish of man, and to lead the repentance of the Church. We must have vision to read the signs of the times, and then pray for courage to bear the implications of what is revealed. The incarnation of Jesus Christ declares to us that the nearer we come to God the closer we shall know ourselves to be involved in his redemptive and recreative work, while at the same time being part of that which needs to be redeemed. The model of Calvary places the beginning of apostolate in the shadow, in an enclosure of failure very different from what is known as success in the world. This is what the person who prays comes to expect. After all, what would a Christian success look like? A gentle, good person never putting a foot wrong, always with the right word at the right time, kind and patient, a white light surrounding him? The only Christian success of which we can be certain was quite unlike that; he had 'no form nor comeliness . . . no beauty that we should desire him . . . despised and rejected of men, a man of sorrows and acquainted with grief'. In those words Isaiah has caught the essence of it. The pattern of the Christians was betrayed by his friends, condemned by Church and State, died on a gallows between two thieves. That is the measure of Christian success. The Desert Fathers have the sure wisdom which distinguishes illusion from reality. A brother went to the Abbot Pastor and told him he had no more temptations and the Abbot said, 'Go, pray to the Lord to command some struggle to be set up in you, for the soul is matured only in battles – the servant is not

65

greater than his Lord.' This is the apostolate of prayer: weakness and strength, failure and success, joy and sorrow; these things do not compete or conflict, rather they are two sides of the same reality of the cross and the resurrection.

CHAPTER FIVE

The Common Mind

A man who is religious, is religious morning, noon and night; his religion is a certain character, a mould in which his thought, words and actions are cast, all forming parts of one and the same whole. He sees God in all things; every course of action he directs towards those spiritual objects which God has revealed to him; every occurrence of the day, every event, every person met with, all news which he hears, he measures by the standards of God's will. And a person who does this may be said almost literally to pray without ceasing; for, knowing himself to be in God's presence, he is continually led to address him reverently, whom he sets always before him in the inward language of prayer and praise, of humble confession and joyful trust.

> J. H. Newman, 'Mental Prayer' in
> *Parochial and Plain Sermons*

The Christian tradition of prayer is one of great moral and spiritual richness. It is still lived by many in their ordinary lives. There is no double standard for those who are priests or who are cloistered, or for the Christian laity who live their commitment to Christ in the secular state. Christian prayer is essentially an extension of Jesus' commission to the apostles, 'Go, therefore, make disciples of all the nations.' By prayer, the Christian pursues no course of escapism but enters into the heart of conflict. Nowhere is this more true than when the Christian is united with Christ in the eucharistic sacrifice, where he is strengthened to bear witness by his sacramental feeding on the body and blood of Christ.

Prayer is the unifying focus of all modes of the Christian life, and through it we catch a vision of the unity of the world. The unity of all Christians is through baptism into the death and resurrection of Christ, with the effect that Christ lives in each one of us. All Christians, whether religious or secular, are called to sanctification. The Christian life may be manifested in many forms, but it is one in its acknowledgement of a total commitment of its members to the service of God. There must be room to breathe in what might be called the novitiate of prayer, to enable the baptismal life to assume its true dimension in the depths of the soul. It is for this reason that the context of prayer should be natural and in no way artificial. Individuality has always been a rich source of life for the Church, for through freedom in praying men have discovered the authentic source of a true Christian spirituality in their own particular field. Yet the heart of the great tradition of prayer is the liturgy, gathering together our common foundations of scripture, the teaching of the Fathers, and an unbroken chain of spirituality reaching back to Cassian, Maximus the Confessor, Simeon the Theologian, Irenaeus, Ignatius the Martyr, and ultimately to the New Testament writings. Christian prayer is a process of constant recovery of our common roots, a pilgrimage which searches ever forward through the tradition of the past. We have suffered so long from over-complications arising from systems of prayer, that many of us have forgotten how to breathe freely, to let in both the illumination and the simplification of the Holy Spirit to show us that prayer must be experienced as one whole, an ever increasing knowledge and submission of the human will to the will of God. Contemplative prayer is open to all, because it is the fruit of baptismal indwelling, a gift freely given and bestowed, requiring us to pay the cost of purification.

There is a difference, however, between the call to contemplative prayer and the call to the contemplative life. Contemplative prayer can be experienced, if God wills it, in any such circumstances as he sees fit to bestow, while contemplative life is the life so directed in its simplicity, and separated from the normal distraction of the active world, that it provides the best preparation for carrying out the work of contemplative prayer. For the contemplative community the work of prayer is the expression of their charity.

The Christian life is a unity in baptism. There is no double standard of higher or lower vocations, there is no praying minority in an otherwise activist Church, no religious priesthood and professional religious with a secularized laity, no specialized prayer for specialized people. There is only the unity of prayer, the gift of God available for all as he wills. As we all face together in the body of Christ a world that is becoming increasingly de-Christianized, it is essential that we should stand together in the simplicity of our Christian witnesses. The common unity of all Christians in the face of the present situation is of paramount importance now that we are called to confront a world that does not think the Christian language or comprehend the Christian ethos and insight. We must understand this situation and meet it, with no disunity to weaken our common witness or love of God and love of neighbour. In the outpouring of love there is only one life to live – the life of charity; and for all of us it springs from the altar, as we offer and are united in Christ with the Father through the Holy Spirit. United with him we are bound to one another. For some of us this oblation will take us out into the highways and hedges; for some of us in enclosure, no less in contact with the world, though in a different way, oblation will hold the needs of the world to God's mercy for healing; for some of us, it will be in the closeness and discipline of ordinary family living. The recognition that the Christian community is the praying community unites the whole Church to the spiritual bond of charity. It is our bounden duty and responsibility to sound the trumpet clearly with no un-certain note. The things which are and the things which are to come, where they are Christian, depend not on the temporal but on the realism of the Christian's assent to the ultimate purposes of God, as they are being worked out through the divine compassion in the successive de-velopment of human history. We must not be discouraged if in the world as it is we find that the Christian Church is in a minority everywhere and in every nation. It is not a question of adjustment or defining ideas to meet the passing situation, but the clear affirmation of the Gospel and of man's incorporation in the action of God through baptism and the maintenance of Christian practice.

In our present climate, this can mean a considerable amount of loneliness. One of the great dilemmas of the twentieth-century technological society is that never be-fore in the history of mankind has there been a time when people have found it so difficult to be alone and so easy to be lonely. Yet being alone does not constitute being lonely. To be lonely is to be deprived of a sense of belonging and of being wanted. It is possible to be lonely in a crowd of people at a football match. It is of course equally possible to be lonely when one lives by oneself without much contact with one's fellow-men, if one is destitute of that inner resourcefulness which is itself the strength in which many people live.

Christians become conscious of their aloneness in the silence of their prayer. When people are lonely they often try to drown their fear and sense of separation by making or listening to a lot of noise. Christians try to learn through silence to come to a true and growing relationship with God and with one another. It is a sobering fact that it is possible for a group of people, especially if they are English, to live at close quarters for a long time and yet not know each other. We don't, in fact, have to be talking all the time to come to know each other quite quickly: a strong bond of mutual understanding and charity can be forged through silence. Seen in this perspective, the Christian, like the solitary sailor, chooses aloneness as part of a personal quest. Christians are people engaged on a search, not only a search for God, though it is always that, but a quest which brings us to a place where we are exposed to a deep heart-searching, a listening awareness of the needs of the people around us. In aloneness we learn to share in the emptiness and lostness of modern man. The Christian is therefore never alone in the sense of being alienated from humanity, unaware of its sorrows and agonies, or unmindful of his responsibilities to bring them, known and unknown, to the mercy of God through prayer. The praying Christian is often alone, but always in the knowledge of the interdependence of all mankind, regardless of race and colour, age or creed. It is therefore essential that we realize the positive use and value of being alone. It is equally valuable for the busy housewife, whose family is at school or at work all day, for the old-age pensioner whose active life has ended, for the commuter driving home through the rush-hour in his car or on the bus. It is true for everyone:

No one of us lives, and equally no one of us dies, for himself alone. If we live, we live for the Lord; and if we die, we die for the Lord. Whether therefore we live or die, we belong to the Lord.

Romans 14:7,8 (N.E.B.)

Many people think that living and dying for God is one thing, living and dying for each other another; but the Christian truth is that in our love of God is contained our love of men. All things offered by us through Christ to the Father, whether in solitude or not, have their place in the divine plan, and in a dimension such as this the concept of being alone is rich with promise, while the idea of loneliness ceases to have dread. The purest alone-ness is the eremitical way of life. The hermit desires to return to the ascesis of silence and to explore the deepest levels of prayer. This is only a question of degree, how-ever, and the personal search for the encounter of the depths of human need in prayer is an immediate possi-bility for any Christian.

This sense of aloneness through the silence of prayer enables us to listen to God and to listen to community, and in this double listening we give a common focus to the two commandments to love God and to love our neighbour. Loving God must flow into love of neighbour; and to love one's neighbour without loving God is simply not possible if one has a true knowledge and understand-ing of the depths of God's love. Living as members of a community asks of us a closer identification with each other as persons who have learned to listen with sensitiv-ity and mutual compassion. That is the real meaning of community, whether it be that of a parish, or university, school, convent or family. Our ability to make a com-munity depends on our readiness to listen to each other.

It depends on our being open and receptive. It depends especially on our being ready to listen to and learn things that are unexpected and new to our experience. It means being ready to learn from frustrations as well as from happiness, from experiences that seem to be negative, as well as the positive ones. It means being ready to question oneself and to re-examine one's past experiences. We continue all through our lives in the discovery of the truth about ourselves through listening to God in prayer and through listening to others, discerning where lie our strengths and our weaknesses, whether we function best in small or large groups, whether we tend to take charge or to opt out, whether or not we are able to exercise authority:

Now, the word 'ascended' implies that he also descended to the lowest level, down to the very earth. He who descended is no other than he who ascended far above all heavens, so that he might fill the universe. And these were his gifts: some to be apostles, some prophets, some evangelists, some pastors and teachers, to equip God's people for work in his service, to the building up of the body of Christ. So shall we all at last attain to the unity inherent in our faith and our knowledge of the Son of God – to mature manhood, measured by nothing less than the full stature of Christ. We are no longer to be children, tossed by the waves and whirled about by every fresh gust of teaching, dupes of crafty rogues and their deceitful schemes. No, let us speak the truth in love; so shall we fully grow up into Christ. He is the head, and on him the whole body depends. Bonded and knit together by every constituent joint, the whole frame grows through the due activity of each part, and builds itself up in love.

Ephesians 4:9-16 (N.E.B.)

Community life, above all else, forces us to live at close quarters with others. We cannot easily escape from those living around us, nor they from us, and any attempt to do so will be obvious to all. We are confronted with the less as well as the more admirable features of ourselves and of our neighbours, and we must learn to live with them. So we learn to be generous towards both our own peculiarities and those of others. This is a perpetual challenge to tolerance, fairness, open-hearted listening and compassion. We are challenged not only in our own personal relationships but by all that we find imperfect in the institutions in which we live and in the methods of those who run them. Here too, there is a great need to practise acceptance and understanding.

From the first, therefore, the interplay of relationship between God and each other requires that we cherish no illusions about our limitations. We should face the fact that authority in community is sometimes exercised by muddle-headed people who have surprisingly little control over the persons and events they ostensibly direct. If we can grasp this fact early on in community life, it will save us much unproductive anger and disappointment. At the same time, if we really grow in openness and listening sensitivity to each other, then, within the apparent limitations of our situation, we shall have considerable opportunity for freedom and joy in relationships as well as great responsibility for each other. It is well known, of course, that one of the great difficulties of leadership is to have to deal with people who will not accept the responsibility of their freedom because they have not learned to build up habits of sensitive listening. The only way to achieve this is by fixing the eyes and ears not on each other but on God as we go forward, a group of persons drawn together by the same voice requiring the

74

attention of each and all. 'Speak, Lord, for your servant hears,' said the child Samuel when God called him by name. He was called, and he heard, and he listened and responded. In all our religious life we should have the same movement of the Spirit operating in us. The basis of any Christian community is not merely a common code of behaviour, or rule, a common way of life, or even shared experience, but the divine call which is addressed both corporately and individually to all its members, and which creates a common mind. The praying Christian community has confidence in its capacity to be renewed both corporately and in its individual members.

If we are to understand maturity in the life of prayer we must consider the meaning of maturity in man; the realization of the full maturity of human life, not a new brand of man, the product of a double standard, but redeemed man who is being formed into what God the creator intended him to be. True religious maturity is attained chiefly by the incorporation in depth of the individual into a common life and purpose, and by his growth and increase in prayer, both the corporate prayer of the Christian community and personal prayer. A community is an organic society, an adult family, created by God to explore and fulfil particular functions within the total Christian body, and to be a prefiguration of the Kingdom of God. In this way the Christian community has a certain element of prophetic anticipation and is a real witness of the whole Church in the life to come. Its true character is pneumatic: it is a Spirit-bearing body, witnessing to more than the natural and bringing the power of the Spirit into the world. In terms of daily living this corporateness demands from the individual a measure of disinterested self-giving, freely willed and offered, not conditioned by rule and custom but arising from a genuine appreciation of and identification with the common mind of the community. In practice, this means that any work undertaken by the Christian can never be merely the expression of his or her own creativeness; it will be the overflow of the corporate purpose in which all participate and which should be of common concern to all.

Christian maturity must therefore be seen in terms both of the corporate and of the individual, for the common mind will be realized only if both the community and its members are tending towards a full adult maturity. Just as a community is greater than the sum total of its members, so the common mind is not a consensus of individual opinions, but a unity of perception which is the fruit of waiting on the Spirit and of mutual openness to each other. Individual opinions are enlarged and deepened and come to full fruition not by force or argument but by common enlightenment. For the realization of this common mind, mature relationships within the community are essential, founded on recognition both of the giving of each individual in the community to the others, and of our need of each other for complete fulfilment of God's purpose. The responsibility of the parish or any other manifestation of the Christian family is to provide a strong, living and loving corporateness (no chilly correctness) into which each individual can give himself and, by so giving, in time be truly sanctified. In the long term, the Christian life is a preparation for eternity, but the short-term process in responding to the will of God must be to secure purity of heart. This purity of heart, which is the end of all forms of Christian life, is something early monasticism took for granted. It is realized by the redirection of our natural powers and creativeness into channels leading Godward, determined and secured by the spirit of commitment, from which flows charity to all mankind. Unless there is a core of community there is no life into which to draw those who are seeking the Christian wholeness; nor are they presented with the challenge by which their aspiration will grow and be fulfilled.

Thus the problem of life in community is, and always will be, the problem of community and individual alike, each growing towards a fuller identity. Full maturity for both will be realized only within the ambit of a certain amount of conflict. Patching a torn garment usually makes the garment weaker, and adherence to the most perfect codes and statutes of organized corporate life will not of itself create unity or guarantee corporate or individual perfection. Renewal and unity, without which there cannot be maturity, must come from within the community, freely willed by each Christian, with each Christian prepared to face the cost of the perfecting of both the corporate and his own personal purification and integration in obedience to the Christian community. The search for God and the attainment of his eternal purpose is the motive of all Christian commitment, and the goal can be achieved only together. We cannot separate our relationship with God from our relationship with our fellow-men. Taken seriously, the Christian life will take us through formal prayer to a deep relationship where in silence and solitude we meet God, and in him become conscious of our coinherence in man's needs and sufferings. Through the modern media of communication and travel there is an ever expanding identification, not merely physical but also psychic, with the needs of everyone throughout the world. This knowledge must be directed into and held by the conscious prayer of those who are channels of God's redemptive love, which is the essence of intercessory prayer. Not that prayer in common should be seen in opposition to deeper solitary prayer, but rather as complementary to it. In the rhythm of our prayer, as in the natural rhythm of our physical life as we pass through adolescence to full maturity, we may find that at times our prayer will require more silence and withdrawal than shared prayer, while at other times the reverse will be true.

In both solitary and common prayer there is the desire to move away from surface impressions to deeper personal experiences, to move beyond an impersonal prayer life, whether individual or communal, and to extend this personal contact with God outwards. When we move away from impersonal, formal meditation, it is to encounter the Holy Trinity, wherein the Father brings forth the Son, and the Son loves the Father in the bond of love which is the Spirit. Indeed, the Trinity is yet again the pattern for the relationship of singleness and plurality, individual and community which creates the tension and unity of the common mind. The fruits of Christian living in the local community, then, are fertilized by a constant renewal in prayer; and the constant renewal in prayer, both individually and corporately, leads us closer to reconciliation in the world. This disposition of prayer depends on givenness, an openness to Christ in us, and for this it is not essential to have a chapel, or a holy corner, or a lighted candle as a focal point, though any of those might help. If we are to live in prayer we must first let Christ pray in us, giving him pride of place. Through that we shall come to understand that loving one's neighbour is not simply being tolerant of or liking him, but recognizing in the neighbour the uniqueness of his place in God's creation, loving him at once as an individual and as a part of the larger community of God. Love of one's neighbour is the joyful knowledge that God is working as uniquely in others' lives as we have experienced him in our own.

This is a period in which every part of human activity is in a phase of crisis – economic, political, philosophical and religious. The foundations of Christian thought and revelation are being laid bare amid contradictory interpretations, and many people are hesitating to commit themselves to traditional forms of religious observance. More than ever, therefore, prayer must not be put forward as a technique to be mastered by the few, but rather as the heritage of all, the essential means of living the Christian life and coming to that personal union with God for which we were created. It is a disturbing fact that these days we frequently find that the true God-seekers, with a hunger and thirst for guidance in silence and the reality of prayer, are to be found outside the orbit of institutional religion. All the more do we need to be very clear that in our own concepts of renewal we do not lose the spirit of silence just because the old traditional forms of devotion seem to be outmoded. The Christian can rightly be grateful both for the scepticism of the scientific temper and for what the scientific and the psychological methods have discovered about the nature of the human personality. The modern Christian can approach both his study of the relevance of religion and also his practice of prayer in the light of such criticism and information. At the same time, or perhaps, following on by way of reaction to the scientific and psychological ethos of our era, there has emerged a widespread interest in the foundations of Christian spirituality. While it is no bad thing to be concerned about the riches that sages have acquired by the rivers of India, it is folly to ignore the revelation of God by the banks of the Jordan, and it is probably unwise to mix the waters indiscriminately, though each stream of spirituality might clarify the other.

We have an increasing need not only in our prayer but also in our actions to become unified and simplified. This is the proper construction of the perceptions of memory and imagination which gathers our whole being to the point where God is no longer an object exterior to ourselves but one who is intimately present with us. Through this new dimension a whole new world can open up to us, and faith becomes a living reality. We are called to explore the depths in ourselves, in other people and in the whole of our society, and in discovering them we need to see that these are not separate depths. This is the century of two world wars, of Hiroshima, of Belsen, of unprecedented torture of body and corruption of minds. The huge cracks in the surface of human behaviour continue to be revealed, while the immense increase in communications means that we are all aware, as never before, of the evils perpetrated by mankind. We meet these all the time, and they can be paralysing. What is even more alarming is that we discover the same roots of violence, frustration, despair within ourselves. Praying in depth means an increase in the understanding of these dark areas in ourselves and in mankind so that they can be held up steadily to the love of God, the only force which can redeem them. When the evil in each one of us is brought before the mercy of God a small part of mankind is also there. When Christians, as men and women of this torn and anguished world, come to stand before God who is our life, all creation begins through us to receive again the gift of life. That is the witness of reconciliation which begins in prayer, bears fruit in action and which requires us to repeat the witness again and again at a level deeper each time. In the Christian life the moment of fulfilment

80

is the moment of renewal. Prayer begins and ends in the inescapable necessity of a relationship with God; the dimension of silence reveals that praying is not only an action, but a still contemplation; the path of spiritual progress is to discern in the union of action and contemplation a deeper listening, through which are heard more clearly the cries of the world, and which leads to an apostolate of prayer renewing the action of reconciliation. The Christian community grows into a common mind of reconciliation, the Church of Reconciliation unites all manner of Christian living, and leads to what is at once a fulfilment and a renewal of our search for complete maturity in ourselves, with each other in the corporateness of our common search, and ultimately with God himself. It is all his work.